T0274925

THE
EXPLORER
AND THE
JOURNALIST

THE
EXPLORER
AND THE
JOURNALIST

FREDERICK COOK, PHILIP GIBBS AND
THE SCANDAL THAT SHOCKED THE WORLD

RICHARD EVANS

The
History
Press

For Evelyn and Orson

Front cover images, clockwise from top left: Frederick Cook (from *The World's Work*, (New York: May 1909), p.565); Philip Gibbs (courtesy of the Gibbs family archive); steamship in ice (iStock.com/ilbusca).
Back cover image: Philip Gibbs interviews Frederick Cook on board the *Hans Egede* (courtesy of the Gibbs family archive).

First published 2023

The History Press
97 St George's Place, Cheltenham,
Gloucestershire, GL50 3QB
www.thehistorypress.co.uk

British Library Cataloguing in Publication Data.
A catalogue record for this book is available from the British Library.

ISBN 978 1 80399 193 1

Typesetting and origination by The History Press
Printed and bound in Great Britain by TJ Books Limited, Padstow, Cornwall.

Trees for Life

CONTENTS

1

A SPELL UPON A MAN

When Philip Gibbs arrived for work in the *Daily Chronicle*'s newsroom on the morning of Friday, 3 September 1909, he was called over by his news editor, Ernest Perris. As he walked to Perris's desk, he had no idea the assignment waiting for him would change the course of his life and become a story told in the pubs of Fleet Street for generations of journalists to come.

Perris was an amateur boxer, a large man with big fists and a reputation for leaving sub-editors bloody nosed after sparring sessions. He was also one of the best news editors in Fleet Street, Gibbs describing him as 'very human in quiet times, though utterly inhuman, or rather super-human, when there was a world scoop in progress'.[1] But that morning, the *Chronicle* had already fallen behind its competitors in its reporting of one of the biggest news stories in years.

Two days earlier, on 1 September, the world had been stunned by the news that American explorer Frederick A. Cook had become the first person to reach the North Pole. This was the golden age of polar exploration, and all the world's leading newspapers scrambled to send reporters to board boats and trains for Copenhagen, where Cook's boat was expected to arrive. All the world's leading newspapers, that is, except the *Daily Chronicle*. For reasons that have never been explained, a day and a half after the news had broken the paper had still not despatched a journalist to Copenhagen. But now it had changed its mind.

Perris told Gibbs to collect a bag of gold coins for expenses, take the razor and toothbrush he kept at the office, and leave for Copenhagen immediately.

'Lots of other men have the start on you,' said Perris, 'but see if you can get some kind of story.'

Gibbs groaned. Going to Copenhagen would mean leaving his wife, Agnes, and their young son, Anthony, for who knows how many days. He also had no interest in polar exploration, knowing so little about it that he spent the boat journey repeating the name 'Dr Cook' to himself to make sure he remembered it, and thinking blackly that he would not even know what to ask Cook in the unlikely event that he managed to speak to him.

Perris probably chose Gibbs for the assignment because of his ability as a descriptive writer. Born in London in 1877, Gibbs had a passion for writing instilled in him at an early age by his father, a civil servant whose love of literature was so infectious that four of his nine children became novelists. Gibbs would always cherish childhood memories of his father reciting poetry to him as they walked down country lanes, and of dinners with him at the Whitefriars Club, where Gibbs met fascinating-seeming men who earned their living through writing.

Gibbs was 15 when he first thought that he, too, might be a professional writer, after something he had written was complimented by John Francis Bentley, the architect of Westminster Cathedral, whose children Gibbs was friends with.[2] He had his first newspaper article published the following year, the *Daily Chronicle* paying him 7*s* 6*d* for a vignette describing seagulls screaming over London Bridge on a winter's afternoon, and he followed this by writing some fairy tales that were published in *Little Folks* magazine. Then, after getting a job in the illustration department of a publishing company, he persuaded his employers to publish his first book, *Founders of the Empire*, which sold well and was used as a textbook in schools.

He was then appointed editor of a literary syndicate in Bolton, where he secured the rights and marketed the work of writers including Arthur Conan Doyle and Rudyard Kipling. While in Bolton, he also wrote a syndicated column that was published in newspapers across the country. The column was good enough to attract the attention of the *Daily Mail*'s brilliant but mercurial founder Alfred Harmsworth.

In 1902, Harmsworth invited Gibbs to London, and at the end of their meeting offered him a job as the *Daily Mail*'s literary editor. This marked the beginning of a career in Fleet Street that Gibbs soon found himself completely absorbed by. 'Fleet Street puts a spell upon a man,'[3] he wrote, describing it as 'one of the best games in the world for any young man with quick eyes, a sense of humour, some touch of quality in his use of words, and curiosity in his soul for the truth and pageant of our human drama, provided he keeps his soul unsullied from the dirt'.[4]

But, as bewitching as he found what he called the 'Spell of the Street', the seven years he had spent in journalism by the time he came to report on the Frederick Cook story had been ones filled with false starts and disappointments, with all four of his previous jobs ending unhappily. His bad luck started on his very first day at the *Daily Mail*, when he arrived at the office – after uprooting his family from Bolton to London – only for Harmsworth to tell him he had forgotten offering him the job, and that he had instead appointed another journalist, Filson Young, as the *Mail*'s literary editor. There followed an awkward conversation where Gibbs reluctantly agreed to work as Young's deputy.

Luckily, Gibbs and Young got on well enough to make the arrangement work and, when Young moved on, Gibbs was finally made literary editor. But his tenure did not last long. One day, Harmsworth invited him to lunch and told him he was secretly planning to launch a literary syndicate and he wanted Gibbs to run it for him. Harmsworth's plan was for Gibbs to go back to the office that afternoon, announce he had been sacked, then go on holiday to the Riviera for a few months. By the time he got back, the syndicate would be ready.

Gibbs was shocked by the suddenness of the proposal and asked for a few days to think about it. But even as the words left his mouth, he saw Harmsworth's face fill with disappointment.

'You're a cautious young man,' Harmsworth said. Coming from someone who had become vastly wealthy through a series of bold decisions, it was not a compliment. Harmsworth immediately cooled on the idea, and shortly afterwards began criticising Gibbs's work. Then, one day, Gibbs overheard one of the *Mail*'s editors criticise him to Harmsworth and saw Harmsworth respond with an ominous nod. Anxious to avoid the indignity of being sacked, Gibbs went upstairs and wrote a letter of resignation, giving it to a messenger boy to take downstairs. Half an hour later, a man arrived in his room and introduced himself to Gibbs as the new literary editor.

Suddenly out of work, Gibbs managed to get a job at the *Daily Express*, but this came to an end after he refused its owner's instruction to write a series of articles proving Francis Bacon was the real author of what he termed 'the so-called Shakespeare plays'. He then found a job at the *Daily Chronicle*, writing articles describing life in England and managing a team of three artists whose illustrations accompanied his descriptions. But he joined at a time when the *Chronicle* was starting to phase out using drawings in favour of photographs, and so it closed his department and made him redundant.

Undaunted, in 1906 he landed the job of literary editor at the *Tribune*, a new newspaper that was about to launch with a big budget and even bigger ambitions to transform British journalism. Gibbs's own budget was so large that he was able to publish the work of writers of the calibre of Rudyard Kipling, Joseph Conrad, and G.K. Chesterton. But for all its ambition, the *Tribune* was doomed from the start by the fact that its array of well-paid journalists was too expensive for it to have any realistic chance of ever breaking even, and the journalism they produced proved too highbrow for advertisers' tastes. After month after month of haemorrhaging money, the owner pulled the plug and it closed in 1908.

On the evening it shut its doors for good, Gibbs stood outside the office with his friend Randal Charlton, sadly watching its green lights go out for the last time. Unemployed again, Gibbs decided to write a novel about Fleet Steet that would tell the story of a fictionalised *Tribune*, and have as its hero a character based on the foppish and unworldly Charlton. He rented a coastguard's cottage in Littlehampton for a month, hoping it would give him the solitude to be able to focus on his writing. But he and Agnes arrived to find that it was next to a funfair, and so he spent his time there writing to the sound of a loud, blaring noise and children's excited screams. Despite the noise, after a month of working late into the night he had produced a novel that he hoped had captured the chaos and exhilaration of life as a daily newspaper journalist in Edwardian Britain.

Now 32, Gibbs was trying to find a publisher for *Street of Adventure* when he got the chance to return to the *Daily Chronicle*, this time as a special correspondent. This meant he would now be focusing on news rather than the descriptive writing and literary criticism that had been his Fleet Street career so far. As well as lacking experience of writing news, there was good reason to think Gibbs's temperament was unsuited to the tough and competitive world of news journalism.

A fellow journalist captured the essence of Gibbs's personality when he wrote that 'his broad brow, his pale, finely chiselled face, thin, sensitive lips, and big clear eyes, show something of the thinker, idealist, and poet that he is by nature'.[5] G.K. Chesterton wrote that Gibbs's 'fine falcon face, with its almost unearthly refinement, seemed set in a sort of fastidious despair'.[6] As a child, he had been so painfully shy that he had been unable to stop himself from blushing if someone used coarse language in his presence. He was also unusually sensitive – he would later remember lacking the 'armour to protect myself against the brutalities, or even the unkindness, of the rough world about me', and feeling the suffering of others so deeply that he would spend hours agonising over the fates of characters in novels.

So he hardly seemed a natural-born newshound, and his unsuitability seemed to be confirmed by his lack of the one quality every good reporter needs – a hunger for exclusive news. Gibbs even thought the chasing of exclusives was almost unseemly. 'On the whole, I don't much believe in the editor or reporter who sets his soul on "scoops", because they create an unhealthy rivalry for sensation at any price – even that of the truth,' he wrote, 'and the "faker" generally triumphs over the truth-teller, until both he and the editor who encouraged him come a cropper by being found out.'[7] In *Street of Adventure*, Gibbs seemed to acknowledge that this lack of hunger for news made him an unlikely news reporter. When the editor of the novel's newspaper talks about what makes a good reporter, he dismisses the value of imagination and literary ability, instead imploring the gods of journalism to 'bring me the man who can smell out facts'.[8]

As Gibbs sat on the boat carrying him towards Copenhagen and one of the biggest stories of the new century, there was nothing to indicate that he might be such a man. But if a journalist fails to seek out news, sometimes news comes to them unbidden. And so it was with Philip Gibbs.

2

AMONG THE WORLD'S GREAT MEN

From the vantage point of a time when mankind has stood on the Moon and launched probes that have sent back images from billions of miles away, it is difficult to grasp just how astonishing the idea of reaching the North Pole seemed to the world of 1909.

The North Pole had held a special place in our collective imagination for hundreds of years, and as the centuries passed and the globe slowly revealed its secrets, it was one of the few places that remained stubbornly unknowable. And the longer it stayed beyond humanity's reach, the more humanity dreamed of the secrets it might hold. It was said to contain an abyss that ships could be pulled into, or iron mountains so magnetic that they could pull nails out of ships. Some even thought it might be a tropical paradise that was home to a lost civilisation.

It featured repeatedly in nineteenth-century literature – Charles Dickens and Wilkie Collins's play *The Frozen Deep* is set in the Arctic, and it is near the Pole that the doctor pursues the monster in Mary Shelley's *Frankenstein*. Polar exploration also features in the work of Jane Austen, Charlotte Brontë, Arthur Conan Doyle, Jules Verne, and many, many more.[1]

At the same time as writers were creating the North Pole of their imaginations, explorers were heading north to try to reach the real thing. The British explorer William Edward Parry set a new record for 'farthest north' in 1827, which stood for almost half a century before being beaten in 1876 by British naval officer Albert Markham, who got within 400 miles of the Pole, celebrating the achievement with whisky and cigars and the singing of 'God Save the Queen'. Markham wrote that he had reached 'a higher latitude, I predict, than will ever be attained',[2] but six years later his record was beaten by members of an expedition led by the American Adolphus Greely, though Greely's expedition ended in tragedy as 18 of its 25 members died of starvation and some of the survivors resorted to cannibalism.[3] The Norwegian explorers Fridtjof Nansen and Hjalmar Johansen made it even closer to the Pole in 1895, and in 1900 the Italian Umberto Cagni claimed the record by getting within 250 miles of it.

The exploits of Arctic explorers were followed avidly by the public, with books about their expeditions often becoming best-sellers. 'There are no tales of risk and enterprise in which we English, men, women, and children, old and young, rich and poor, become interested so completely, as in the tales that come from the North Pole,' the journalist Henry Morley wrote in 1853.[4] Like the Moon landing many years later, the reason the public was so gripped by the idea of reaching the North Pole was not so much because of what might be found there, but because of what it seemed to say about the human spirit. And each expedition further added to the Pole's mystique, the failures reinforcing its sense of danger and the successes increasing the public's belief that the dream of reaching it might now be achievable. 'May the day at least not be far off,' wrote the Duke of Abruzzi, who had led the expedition on which Cagni had broken the record, 'when the mystery of the Arctic regions shall be revealed, and the names of those who have sacrificed their lives to it shine with still greater glory'.[5]

Then, on 1 September 1909, a ship called the *Hans Egede* made an unscheduled stop at Lerwick in the Shetland Islands, and the ship's officer rowed ashore with an American explorer called Frederick A. Cook. When they reached the shore, they walked to the town's one-room telegraph station and sent five telegrams, all of them containing a single message – that mankind's long, long quest to reach the North Pole was finally complete.

In newspaper offices around the world, shocked journalists sat down to write articles in which they tried to do justice to the magnitude of the news they were reporting. 'It is difficult to find words adequate to express the stupendous significance of an event which ends a quest that has gone on steadily for so many scores of years and levied its toll on so many men,' the *Manchester Guardian* reported. In France, *Le Petit Parisien* welcomed the 'astounding news' and *Le Matin* told its readers that 'for the last five centuries the efforts of explorers have rushed to the arctic extremity of the world ... and it is America which emerges triumphant in this heroic journey'.[6]

The *London Daily News* reported that 'with intensely dramatic suddenness the report that an American, who had long been given up for dead, had reached the North Pole, burst on the world yesterday,' while *The Times* thought that 'if the story is confirmed, [Cook] will be enrolled among the world's great men'.[7] *The New York Times* compared his achievement to Columbus's 'discovery' of the Americas, arguing that 'humanity would rank with that great voyager the man who shall have set foot on Earth's chill and profitless extremity'.[8] Philip Gibbs's *Daily Chronicle* was just as effusive, declaring 'all honour to the daring man who, having been given up for dead, has appeared with the news of victory', and telling its readers that 'it seems that what appeared to be the unattainable has been attained, and that, after a thousand years or more of perilous adventure, the Pole itself has at last been conquered!'[9]

Journalists also sought the reaction of the world's leading explorers. The Duke of Abruzzi declared it 'the greatest achievement of the twentieth century',[10] and Anthony Fiala, an American explorer who had spent two years stranded in the Arctic after his own failed polar attempt, said Cook 'deserves immense credit for his brilliant success'.[11] Cook's friend Roald Amundsen, who would later become the first person to reach the South Pole, heaped praise on him. Cook was 'an uncommonly staunch, persevering, and energetic personality, and I admire him', Amundsen told journalists, adding that he thought his dash for the Pole was the 'most brilliant sledge trip in the history of polar exploration'.

The *Daily Mail* got the explorer Ernest Shackleton, who had arrived back in London three months earlier after getting to within 112 miles of the South Pole, to write an article about Cook's achievement. 'Such a journey single-handed would seem to be an almost superhuman effort, and no praise would be too great for so fine a feat of courage and endurance,' Shackleton wrote. 'Dr Cook has succeeded, it seems, where many men have failed, and from the world at large, and from Polar explorers in particular, he will receive the warmest congratulations. I have very recent recollections of hardship and struggle in ice-bound regions, and therefore I can realise what the effort must have cost and feel personal pleasure that it should have been crowned with such magnificent success.'[12]

While explorers such as Shackleton, Amundsen, and Robert Falcon Scott were famous as a result of public fascination with the golden age of polar exploration, Cook had started the day hardly known outside the United States, most people being unaware of his expedition. So that afternoon, journalists also hurriedly researched the story of the man who had suddenly emerged from relative obscurity to claim a place alongside Marco Polo and Christopher Columbus in the pantheon of the very greatest explorers. From old newspaper cuttings and conversations with polar experts, they learned that Cook was a well-respected explorer who had quietly left the United States in June 1907 with a plan to reach the North Pole. He had hoped to be back by September 1908, but September 1908 had come and gone and, after no word from him for over a year, many assumed he was probably dead.

Many leading polar explorers came from relatively affluent families, but as journalists pieced together the details of Cook's background, the picture that emerged of his early life was one of grinding poverty marked by a series of tragedies. The man who had been forged by this upbringing was one whose amiable and unassuming manner hid a resilience and will to succeed that was exceptional even by the extreme standards of polar exploration.

Born in 1865, two months after the end of the Civil War, Cook was the fourth of five children of German immigrants. He grew up in the foothills of New York's Catskill Mountains, his first few years spent in relative comfort thanks to his father's income as a doctor. But his father died when he was 5, and the loss of his salary meant the family's existence was suddenly transformed into a constant struggle to find enough money to pay for food. The family then suffered further tragedy when Cook's sister died of scarlet fever when he was about 15.

In his teenage years, Cook kept a punishing schedule of doing his schoolwork at the same time as holding down part-time jobs to support his family. By the time he left school at the age of 16, the family had moved to New York City and Cook got a job as an office boy and rent collector, saving his earnings until he could afford to buy a printing press, and using it to start a small printing business. He built up the business over the next few years and then sold it, using the money to buy a milk route that he hoped would give him a regular income while he went to medical school. So began an arduous routine of starting work on the milk route at 1 a.m., then going straight to medical school for 9 a.m., and then after a day's studying going home to be in bed for 5.30 p.m., before starting the whole thing again. Not only did he manage to keep going, but he was able to grow the business and still found time to court Libby Forbes, a young woman he met at a temperance festival.

Cook and Libby married in the spring of 1889, and by the end of the year Libby was pregnant. To the 24-year-old Cook, it must have seemed that after his long years of struggle the pieces were finally falling into place for an idyllic life as a doctor with a loving family. But his life was shattered when their baby daughter died shortly after being born, and Libby died of an infection a week later.

Grief-stricken and suddenly alone, Cook threw himself into his work and, now newly qualified as a doctor, he sold the milk business and set up his own medical practice. But attracting patients proved harder than he expected, and the financial worry added to his grief. Around this time, he started reading books by Arctic explorers, finding escape from his sadness and anxiety in their stories of struggling to survive in an alien landscape. And then he read a newspaper article that was to change his life.

The article was about the American explorer Robert Peary, who was planning an expedition to Greenland and was looking for expedition members. Cook would later remember that as he read the article he had felt 'as if a door to a prison cell opened',[13] and that same day he wrote to Peary to offer his services. Peary agreed to appoint him expedition physician, and Cook joined the expedition when it left New York in June 1891. They returned the following September with the triumphant news that they had significantly expanded human knowledge of the world by confirming for the first time that Greenland was an island.

Cook's year in the Arctic had been filled with hardship. A member of the expedition was presumed to have fallen to his death after failing to return from collecting mineral samples, and Cook himself had only survived the collapse of an igloo he was sheltering in because Peary dug him out and then stopped him freezing to death by sheltering him from the wind. But the expedition had also showed Cook that he had a natural aptitude for polar conditions. He was so impervious to the cold that he sometimes chose to sleep outside in temperatures far below freezing, and he proved able to maintain his good humour even when the tempers of the other expedition members became badly frayed. He had also been fascinated by the Inuit they met in Greenland. While many nineteenth-century explorers had a racist attitude towards the Inuit that meant they dismissed them as inferior, Cook developed a deep respect for them and spent long hours studying their diet and customs and learning from them how to drive dogs and build igloos and sledges.

Above all, Cook's time in Greenland had turned his interest in the Arctic into something closer to addiction; he would later write that 'no explorer has ever returned [from the Arctic] who does not long for the remainder of his days to go back'.[14] So when Peary announced his next expedition, Cook agreed to join him. But he withdrew after becoming annoyed with Peary for refusing to let him publish his research on the Inuit before Peary's own book was published. Instead, Cook set off on his own trip to Greenland, and then the following year led an Arctic tourist expedition. But it was beset with problems from the start, and came to a premature end when it hit a reef and had to be rescued by another ship.

The publicity from Cook's Arctic trips meant his medical practice was now doing well, and he again found personal happiness when he fell in love with and got engaged to his late wife's sister, Anna. But he still felt the pull of exploration, spending the last few years of the nineteenth century unsuccessfully trying to raise the funds for his own Antarctic expedition. In 1897, he still had nowhere near enough money for an expedition when he read a newspaper article about the *Belgica*, a Belgian ship that was about to depart for Antarctica. As he had done with Peary six years earlier, Cook immediately wrote to the expedition leader, Adrien de Gerlache, offering his services as a doctor. De Gerlache initially rejected him, but when the *Belgica*'s physician resigned at the last minute, de Gerlache sent Cook another message offering him the role and telling him to meet them in Rio de Janeiro. By this point, Anna had fallen into ill health and Cook was reluctant to leave her, but the lure of exploration was too strong. He said goodbye to her and boarded a ship for Rio, where he met the *Belgica* and its crew of Belgians, Norwegians, a Pole, and a Romanian.

Among the crew was 25-year-old Norwegian Roald Amundsen, then unknown and inexperienced, but already ambitious and hungry to build the skills and knowledge that would lead to him becoming one of the world's greatest explorers. Cook was the only member of the *Belgica* with previous experience of polar exploration, and so Amundsen was drawn to him as someone he could learn from. The two men developed a close friendship, Cook impressing Amundsen with a seemingly never-ending stream of ideas for the future that covered everything from designs for wind-resistant tents and snow goggles to introducing Antarctic animals to the Arctic and using penguin faeces as a fertiliser to solve world hunger.

They went hunting and exploring together, and their friendship was cemented by a dangerous trek they made when they were tied to each other with rope. Climbing a mountain, Amundsen was impressed by the way Cook calmly and methodically cut footholds in the ice despite being so high that any slip would mean falling to his certain death, and by the courage Cook showed in crawling across a sheet of ice that formed a bridge across a crevice, despite not being sure it would hold his weight. A little later, the snow gave way under Cook's feet, and Amundsen had to use all his strength to pull the rope connecting them, so saving both of them from falling to their deaths. Cook returned the favour shortly afterwards when Amundsen suddenly fell through the snow and found himself dangling above a huge drop; Cook managed to hold onto the rope long enough for Amundsen to pull himself back up.[15] Many years later, the lifelong bond between the two men would still be evident when Amundsen remembered Cook's contribution to the *Belgica*: 'He, of all the ship's company, was the one man of unfaltering courage, unfailing hope, endless cheerfulness, and unwearied kindness. When anyone was sick, he was at his bedside to comfort him; when in any way disheartened, he was there to encourage and inspire. And not only was his faith undaunted, but his ingenuity and enterprise were boundless.'[16]

These were characteristics the whole *Belgica* crew came to rely on, as they looked to Cook to help them through an expedition that at times became a living nightmare. Just eight days after leaving Isla de los Estados off the southern tip of South America in January 1898, the *Belgica* was hit by tragedy when the 20-year-old Norwegian Carl Wiencke fell into the sea. Cook tried to save Wiencke by pulling a line Wiencke had managed to grab hold of, but he slowly felt Wiencke's grip loosen and then stood horror-stricken with the rest of the crew as they watched him die in the freezing water.

Following Wiencke's death, the expedition tried to focus on the task ahead of them, spending the next few weeks collecting flora and fauna and geological samples. As they did so, they were frequently left open-mouthed by the vast swathes of new Antarctic land they discovered containing some of the most beautiful scenery on Earth. 'Everything about us had an other-world appearance,' Cook wrote about their first landing. 'The scenery, the life, the clouds, the atmosphere, the water – everything wore an air of mystery.' But in February, they were forced to become the first people to spend a winter in Antarctica after their ship became stuck in ice (it is now thought de Gerlache did this deliberately, but he kept this from the others).

Living through an Antarctic winter meant enduring two months of continuous darkness, freezing cold temperatures, and the constant fear that their ship would be crushed by the ice. The experience took a great mental and physical toll. The health of most expedition members deteriorated alarmingly – one of them died of heart failure and another was left so mentally disturbed that he spent the rest of his life in an institution. It was largely down to Cook that things were not even worse. He took his physician duties incredibly seriously, diligently interviewing every crew member to understand their mental state and organising skiing trips to encourage them to exercise. And when the crew grew listless and tired and started experiencing headaches and fluctuating heart rates, Cook was perceptive enough to recognise the early signs of scurvy. Remembering that the Inuit he had met in Greenland had not suffered from scurvy, he wondered if there was something in their diet of fresh meat that prevented it, and so he ordered the ship's crew to eat fresh penguin and seal meat instead of the canned food they had been living on. It was a moment of brilliance that almost certainly saved lives.

And when the long Arctic night finally lifted and the *Belgica* celebrated the sun's return, it was Cook who drove the crew on to find a way to escape the ice. The other expedition members had a fatalistic attitude to the ice, believing it to be so strong that they had no choice but to wait until it freed them. But Cook argued that spending another winter stuck in the ice would inevitably mean more deaths, and so it was their moral duty to do everything they could to try to get free. At first, he was derided as an unrealistic dreamer, Amundsen later remembering that it seemed 'at first like a mad undertaking'.[17] But he eventually persuaded the others to try his idea of digging trenches between the ship and an open basin of water not far away. When the ice finally cracked, Cook thought, it would do so along the lines of the trenches and they would be able to reach the basin, from where they might be able to get to the open sea.

This initial plan did not work, so they instead tried cutting out blocks of ice to create a waterway between them and the basin. When friction meant they were unable to move the blocks they had cut, it was Cook who worked out how to cut the blocks in a shape that would make them easy to remove. After a month of back-breaking work, they had removed enough ice for the *Belgica* to make it to the basin, and in March 1899 they finally reached the open sea after over a year trapped in ice. 'The miracle happened – exactly what Cook had predicted,' Amundsen wrote. 'The ice opened up and the lane to the sea ran directly to our basin!'

The *Belgica* made its way back to South America, where Cook said goodbye to his friends and travelled up to Uruguay, where he received the awful news that his fiancée Anna had died. Her health had apparently improved after he left, but then declined after newspapers reported that the *Belgica* was missing and its crew feared dead.

When he got back to New York, Cook returned to his medical practice, but he also gave lectures about his polar travels, had an article about the *Belgica* published by the *New York Herald*, and wrote a memoir about his time in Antarctica. Called *Through the First Antarctic Night*, it was the first English-language account of the expedition and it received good reviews, helping build Cook's reputation as the only living American who had explored both the Arctic and Antarctic. In 1901, he visited Europe to take part in the Commission de la Belgica that was to prepare the *Belgica*'s data for publication, and while in

Europe he visited London and met both Ernest Shackleton and Captain Robert Falcon Scott.

On Cook's return to the United States, he gave the impression that he had finally got exploration out of his system, telling a journalist that 'I have been exploring for many years now, and I think I'll give someone else a chance'.[18] His medical practice was doing better than ever, and he met and married a wealthy 24-year-old widow called Marie Hunt, writing to Amundsen that their marriage would mean 'my polar adventures will be at an end'. When he married Marie, he also adopted her young daughter, Ruth, and shortly after the wedding Marie gave birth to a baby girl they named Helen.

Now 37, Cook was earning good money and finally had the family life that had been cruelly taken from him with the deaths of his first wife and baby daughter over a decade earlier. But when he was asked to join a relief expedition for Robert Peary, who was in the Arctic and had not been heard from for some time, Cook left his family and boarded a boat for the Arctic. They found Peary in north-western Greenland, where he had spent the last two years on two failed attempts to reach the North Pole. Cook examined him and was alarmed to find that his skin had turned a grey-green colour, his eyes were dull and most of his toes had been lost to frostbite. Worried about Peary's health, Cook urged him to come back to the United States for medical treatment, but Peary insisted on staying for one more try for the Pole, and Cook returned without him.

Cook's life was then changed once again by an article he read, this time about Mount McKinley (now called Denali) in Alaska. It had been confirmed as North America's highest peak five years earlier and no one was known to have reached the top. Because doing so would mean crossing the world's largest glaciers outside of Greenland and Antarctica, Cook thought his experience of this kind of terrain meant it was a challenge he would be ideally suited to.

He first tried to climb McKinley in 1903, but the expedition ended in failure when his party had to turn back after coming to an impassable ridge. By the time they returned to civilisation they were almost starving and their clothes were in rags, but they had at least made history by becoming the first known people to circumnavigate the mountain. Three years later, in 1906, he tried again. One of his group, the 39-year-old Columbia University physicist Professor Herschel Parker, turned back when they were still miles from the top, and others in the party then went off on their own to hunt big game. But Cook and Ed Barrill, a Montanan who was helping with the horses, pressed on, apparently without any hope of reaching the top but wanting to get as far as possible to identify the best route for another attempt the following year. But when they returned, it was with the news that they had made quicker-than-expected progress and had carried on through howling winds and freezing temperatures until, on 16 September 1906, they became the first ever people known to have reached McKinley's summit.

Their conquest of McKinley was front-page news, *The New York Times* reporting that 'Cook's feat is particularly notable, as his is the first ascent of the mountain on record and followed repeated failures'.[19] It was an achievement that confirmed him as one of America's leading explorers. He was elected president of the Explorers Club, asked to lecture at the Association of American Geographers, honoured at the American Alpine Club annual dinner, and was guest of honour at a National Geographic Society banquet. At the Geographic Society event, the inventor Alexander Graham Bell introduced him as 'one of the few Americans, if not the only American, who had explored both extremes of the world', and said his ascent of McKinley meant he had now also 'been to the top of the American continent, and therefore to the top of the world'.[20]

His new-found prestige also led to an approach from the millionaire John R. Bradley, who offered to finance an Arctic expedition where Cook would study the Inuit while Bradley hunted big game. Cook agreed, and they began making preparations. Then in June 1907, just weeks before they were due to leave, they were dining together when Cook asked Bradley if he would be interested in trying for the North Pole.

'Not I,' said Bradley. 'Would you like to try for it?'

'There is nothing I would rather do,' Cook said. 'It is the ambition of my life.'

3

DR COOK, I BELIEVE

It was the evening of Friday, 3 September, by the time Philip Gibbs arrived in Copenhagen, and he was tired and had a headache after travelling all day.

He asked a taxi driver to take him somewhere he could get a strong coffee and write an article for the next day's *Daily Chronicle* and, as the taxi drove him through streets adorned with bunting and countless Danish and American flags that had been put up for Cook's arrival, he thought about the task ahead of him.

Covering a story of this magnitude was a chance to make a name for himself, but the odds seemed stacked against him. He did not speak any Danish, had no contacts in Copenhagen, and did not even know if Cook had arrived in the city yet. He was also arriving a day later than other journalists, and even before he left London another newspaper had published Cook's own account of reaching the North Pole.

It was the *New York Herald* that had secured what was one of the biggest exclusives in newspaper history, and it had come to them through pure luck. Because the *Herald* had published Cook's account of the *Belgica* expedition in 1899, Cook thought it was the obvious newspaper to offer his story of reaching the Pole. So at Lerwick in the Shetland Islands, he had sent the *Herald* a message telling them he was leaving a 2,000-word article at the telegraph office that they could print if they agreed to pay him $3,000. This was a sum the average American would take years to earn, but it represented a bargain for an exclusive account of an era-defining story. The *Herald* quickly agreed, and the next day published his article about how he had reached the Pole under the proud, if overlong, headline, 'The North Pole is discovered by Dr Frederick Cook, who cables to the Herald an exclusive account of how he set the American flag on the world's top'.[1]

Cook had an extraordinary story to tell, and he was a good enough writer to do it justice. His article set out how he had spent the first winter of his trip in north-western Greenland, and how he had led a party of 11 Inuit and 103 dogs as they endured temperatures as low as -83°C. He had then selected two Inuit and 26 dogs for the final 460-mile dash for the Pole, living on pemmican (a mix of dried meat and berries) and keeping their dogs from starving by killing some of them and feeding them to the others. After nine days, they discovered a new land of around 30,000 square miles, and they carried on over ice that contained no signs of life until, finally, on 21 April 1908, Cook's observations confirmed that he and the two Inuit had become the first people to set foot on the North Pole. 'With a single step we could pass from one side of the earth to the other; from midday to midnight,' Cook wrote. 'At last the flag floated to the breezes of the pole ... Although crazy with joy, our spirits began to undergo a feeling of weariness. Next day, after taking observations, a sentiment of intense solitude penetrated us while we looked at the horizon. Was it possible that this desolate region, without a patch of earth, had aroused the ambition of so many men for so many centuries?'

With the *Herald* already having published Cook's account, as Gibbs's taxi arrived at a smoke-filled café it was difficult to see how he could find anything new to say about the story unless he could somehow manage to speak to Cook himself. Gibbs sat down at a table in the café, drinking his coffee and flicking through a Danish newspaper in which the only two words he could understand were repeated throughout: 'Dr Cook'.

The waiter serving him spoke English, and Gibbs asked if Cook had arrived in the city yet.

'No. He ought to have been here at midday. But there's a fog in the Kattegat [the area of sea to the north of Copenhagen] and his boat will not come in until tomorrow morning. All Denmark is waiting for him.'

Gibbs mentioned that he was a journalist.

'There are many journalists here from all countries,' said the waiter. 'They are all anxious to interview the man who has been the first to reach the North Pole. They are waiting in Copenhagen to meet him when he arrives.'

Gibbs thanked him and went back to drinking his coffee and smoking his cigarette, taking some comfort from the fact that at least Cook had not arrived in Copenhagen before him. Perhaps being a day behind the other journalists would not matter, after all.

He was suddenly interrupted in his thinking by a low murmuring, and looked up to see his fellow customers' interest directed towards a woman who had just walked in. She was wearing a white fur cap and a white fox-skin around her neck, and she was with a young woman and a tall man with unkempt hair. As Gibbs watched them take their seats, he had no idea he was looking at one of the biggest lucky breaks any journalist has ever had.

The waiter returned to Gibbs's table.

'Did you see that beautiful lady?' he whispered excitedly. 'That is Mrs Rasmussen!'

Gibbs looked at him blankly, not recognising the name.

'She's the wife of Knud Rasmussen, the famous explorer,' the waiter explained. 'It was he who provided Dr Cook with his dogs before he set out for the North Pole. They are great friends.'

If Mrs Rasmussen's husband was Cook's friend, Gibbs thought, then perhaps she might have information about him. Most journalists would have gone straight over to talk to her, but Gibbs sat smoking his cigarette and looking over at her, struggling to overcome his shyness. But he finally summoned his courage, walked over, and bowed courteously, telling her he was an English journalist who had come to Denmark to try to interview Dr Cook, and he wondered if she might be able to help him. She seemed amused, and they began talking in a mixture of French, German, and English.[2]

She told him her name was Dagmar Rasmussen, and introduced the tall man with her as the Arctic explorer Peter Freuchen, a close friend of her husband who spoke good enough English to be able to help with the translation. As well as being beautiful, the 27-year-old Dagmar Rasmussen came from a wealthy family and was a talented pianist with a love of opera. Gibbs was instantly charmed by her. And while she had no direct news of Cook, she told Gibbs that a boat owned by the Danish-Greenland Company was supposed to be leaving the city of Elsinore early the next day to meet Cook's ship before it reached land. She said that because her husband had been the last person apart from the Inuit to see Cook before his dash for the Pole, she had wanted to be one of the first people to welcome Cook to Denmark, but Elsinore was some 40 miles away and they would not be able to get there in time.

Gibbs suddenly saw an opportunity. 'Surely if you really want to go, it would be excellent to travel to Elsinore tonight, put up at a hotel, and get on board the launch at dawn,' he said. 'If you would allow me to accompany you ...'

Dagmar Rasmussen laughed, telling him the last train to Elsinore had already left.

'Let us have a taxi and drive there!' Gibbs said.

Cars were not allowed to drive outside Copenhagen at night unless they had a special licence, she told him, and breaking the rule might mean a fine or even prison. But Gibbs was insistent, calling over the waiter and asking him to find a taxi driver. A minute later, a taxi driver arrived at their table, cap in hand, and the waiter translated Gibbs's request to drive them to Elsinore. The taxi driver shook his head and said something in Danish, and the waiter explained that he did not want to take them because of the risk of being fined.

'How much, including the fine?' Gibbs asked.

The waiter conferred again with the taxi driver, and then said he would do it for £5. This was the equivalent of hundreds of pounds today, but Gibbs reasoned it was nothing compared to the potential value of an interview with the first man to reach the North Pole. Gibbs turned to the others at the table, asking them if they would come with him. They laughed, and then whispered among themselves.

'But when we get there, supposing you were not allowed on the launch by the director of the Danish-Greenland Company?' asked Dagmar Rasmussen. 'He is our friend. But you are, after all, a stranger.'

'I should have had an amusing drive,' Gibbs said. 'It would be worthwhile. Perhaps you would tell me what Dr Cook says, when you return.'

They hesitated, and then finally agreed to go with him. They waited another hour until 10 p.m., thinking this would make them less likely to run into the police, and while they waited they ate dinner and Gibbs went out to telegraph his article back to London. In this first article from Copenhagen, Gibbs hailed Cook's achievement as 'more striking than any in the history of travel in the past hundred years'. 'Copenhagen is in the height of expectancy of the arrival of Dr Cook, and the city is doing its utmost to mark worthily so great an event as the arrival of the discoverer of the North Pole,' he continued. 'An event of such great international interest has never before occurred in this capital, and the citizens are determined to make the most of it … Probably no explorer ever had such a reception as has been prepared for the intrepid American.'[3]

Gibbs also mentioned his meeting with Dagmar Rasmussen (though he referred to her as 'Mrs Amundsen', obviously confusing her husband with Roald Amundsen). He reported that she did 'not doubt his statement that he has actually reached the Pole', and was on her way to Elsinore to try to meet him.

With his article sent to London and dinner eaten, the group got into the taxi and started for Elsinore, keeping their lights off as they drove through the city to avoid being seen by the police. 'I thought how incredible it was,' Gibbs wrote, 'that I should be sitting there opposite a beautiful lady with a silver fox round her throat, with a laughing girl by her side, and a young Danish explorer next to the driver, riding through Denmark with lights out, to meet a man who had discovered

the North Pole, and whose name I had never heard two days before ...
These things happen only in journalism and romance.'

It was not long before they learned the value of the rule against
driving at night, when they crashed into a cyclist. Peter Freuchen
rushed out to see if the man was OK, and Gibbs stayed in the car, listening anxiously to Freuchen talking in Danish to a crowd that had
gathered. 'How much to pay?' Gibbs shouted, but no one answered
him and Freuchen eventually got back in the car and said there was
nothing to pay because the man was not badly injured. They carried
on with the journey, and despite the taxi driver going at such a speed
that Gibbs later remembered 'there were moments when I thought
that we should all have our necks broken', they reached Elsinore,
famous as the setting for Shakespeare's *Hamlet*, without further incident. They went to a hotel and ordered some hot drinks, and then
Dagmar Rasmussen spotted the director of the Danish-Greenland
Company. Gibbs stayed back while the other three went to talk to
him. His hope of meeting Cook rested on the director, and it was
a hope that faded as he watched their conversation from afar, his
new friends' body language suggesting they were disappointed by
what they were being told. After they finished talking to him, they
returned to Gibbs.

'He won't take us,' said Dagmar Rasmussen.

'Hard luck,' said Gibbs.

'But he will take you.'

She explained that the director had been inundated with requests
from friends for a place on the boat, and so had decided to refuse them
all for fear of appearing to favour some friends over others. But when
they mentioned Gibbs was a journalist, he decided that since there were
already two or three other journalists on the boat, he could give him a
place without causing offence.

Gibbs's companions were gracious about the news and wished him
luck as he boarded a small boat that took him to a ship in the Kattegat
that would meet the *Hans Egede* early the next morning. In his excitement, Gibbs left his coat behind and was freezing by the time they

reached the ship, where he gratefully warmed himself with a cup of cocoa in the captain's cabin.

As dawn broke the next day, Gibbs heard a shout that the *Hans Egede* had been seen, and they steamed towards it until they were alongside it. A rope ladder was lowered and the men in front of Gibbs jumped onto the ladder and climbed up onto the ship. Then it was Gibbs's turn, and he eyed the ladder nervously, thinking that 'if I miss that rope ladder that's the end of my adventure'. He managed to get his foot on it, awkwardly grabbing hold of it and managing to clamber up the ladder and onto the deck.

Waiting to greet the visitors was a man with an untidy moustache wearing a shabby-looking suit. From his prominent nose and striking eyes, Gibbs recognised him from photographs as Frederick Cook.

Gibbs walked up to the explorer who was at the centre of the biggest story in the world and offered his hand, his shyness now forgotten in the euphoria of finding himself on the brink of a huge journalistic coup.

'Dr Cook, I believe,' Gibbs said, as he shook hands with the explorer.

4

THE STORY OF THE WORLD

'I guess you're the first Englishman to give me a greeting,' Cook told Gibbs, warmly shaking his hand.

'Yes,' Gibbs replied, 'and your welcome will be as warm in England as anywhere if you will just answer a few questions and satisfy us on some difficult points.'

'I thought you would begin to ask questions, but I am ready to answer them. Come and have some breakfast, young man.'

They went into the *Hans Egede*'s dining saloon, sitting opposite each other among people who were dressed in furs and had sunburnt faces. 'I was favourably impressed by the first appearance of the man who says he reached the Pole,' Gibbs wrote. 'Here, surely, was a typical sea-rover. Under his Danish cap there was a mass of shaggy fair hair, a pair of smiling blue eyes, and a florid face with a powerful nose and a large mouth which, when he smiled, showed broken teeth. An honest face, surely, if any face is honest.'

All Gibbs could think about was that being alone with the man who discovered the North Pole before he reached Copenhagen was the sort of opportunity most journalists spent their careers dreaming of. Yet at first Cook seemed reluctant to talk about his polar journey. But later, they were joined by two Danish journalists and a few others, and Cook told the story of how he had reached the Pole. This included details he had not mentioned in his *New York Herald* article, and Gibbs and the other journalists eagerly wrote down every word as Cook explained how he had dug holes in the snow to protect himself from the wind, set traps for bears, and had once been so hungry he had eaten a dead seal he had found.[1]

'It was with faint hope of seeing my friends again that I plunged into the land of eternal loneliness, in the winter of endless night,' Cook said, his rapt audience listening in silent awe as he told his story in florid, brilliantly quotable language. 'It was always the same, one day like another, going onwards to the North with nothing in sight upon the great white desert … I had no hours of exciting peril, only the continual risk of death from slow starvation. When at last I reached the North Pole, and when every line was south, and I stood on the summit of the world, I put up a sign that my journey was at an end, and that a victory had been gained for my country.'

Gibbs was not quite the first journalist to speak to Cook. The previous day, a group of reporters had managed to speak to him – it is unclear whether they boarded the *Hans Egede* or shouted questions from another boat – but he had not said anything particularly newsworthy. Then just hours before Gibbs arrived, a *Daily Mirror* reporter had got aboard and interviewed him. Cook told the *Mirror* journalist that as he had approached the Pole he had felt 'acute pleasure which I cannot describe', but by the time he reached it was 'too tired really to feel any sensation'.[2] Even as Gibbs sat talking to Cook, copies of the *Daily Mirror* containing the interview were arriving at newsagents across Britain. But as much as newspapers put a premium on being first with the news, the *Mirror* article would be quickly forgotten, while Gibbs's account of meeting Cook would become part of journalistic legend.

Once Cook had finished his story and answered Gibbs's questions, he went back into his cabin. A little while later, photographers and men with film cameras boarded the boat and Carl Martin Norman Hansen, a 48-year-old Danish explorer and poet who had befriended Cook, went into his cabin to bring him out to pose for the cameras. Then with his publicity duties over, Cook and Norman Hansen stood on the bridge of the *Hans Egede* as they approached Copenhagen's Toldbod Quay, where the welcome waiting for him was of a scale few people arriving in a new city have ever experienced. 'It would be impossible by means of any written description to convey a full impression of the marvellous reception which was given the explorer,' the *Daily Telegraph & Courier* reported. 'It was not a scene of enthusiasm merely, but an enthusiasm wild, foolish, uncontrollable.'[3] There were a reported 50,000 people crammed onto the quayside to see him arrive and the water was crowded with hundreds of boats, many of them flying the Stars and Stripes and blaring their horns, as bands struck up 'See the Conquering Hero Comes'.[4] Gibbs wrote that 'pennants fluttered, sirens shrieked, whistles shrilled over the dancing waters. It was a welcome for a hero by a nation of seamen.'[5]

Gibbs was standing near Cook as they approached the harbour, and he watched his face for a clue as to what he was thinking. 'It had a fixed smile with which I am now familiar,' Gibbs wrote. 'But once or twice a nervous look crept into his eyes, as though he were rather afraid of that enthusiasm which awaited him.' Cook would later remember feeling overwhelmed at the sight of the waiting crowd after two years away from civilisation: 'Like a bolt from the blue there burst upon me the clamour of Copenhagen's ovation. I was utterly bewildered by it … Like a darting army of water bugs innumerable craft of all kind were leaping toward us on the sun-lit water. Tugs and motors, rowboats and sailboats, soon surrounded and followed us. The flags of all nations dangled on the decorated craft. People shouted, it seemed, in every tongue. Wave after wave of cheering rolled over the water.'[6]

Among the crowd was Denmark's Crown Prince Christian, his uncle Prince Valdemar, and the American writer Maurice Egan, who was then serving as the US Minister for Denmark. When the *Hans Egede* reached within a mile of Toldbod Quay, they boarded the royal launch and set off to meet Cook. A gangway was placed between the two boats and the Crown Prince climbed aboard, shaking Cook's hand and congratulating him on behalf of Denmark.

Cook would later remember feeling painfully aware of the contrast between the dignitaries' fine clothes and 'my dirty, soiled, baggedat-the-knees suit'.[7] But if Cook felt cowed by their arrival, it was not apparent to Gibbs. 'I was struck then by the man's simplicity of manner and by his wonderful command over himself,' he wrote. 'He was the bluff sailor man to the Prince, respectful and smiling, but not quick to answer the questions which came from every side.'

'Come ashore with me, please, the people are waiting to see you,' Crown Prince Christian said to Cook, and he led him onto the royal launch that took them the rest of the way to the quay. Cook waved and doffed his cap to the crowd, and as he stepped onto the quay a woman gave him some roses and the crowd pushed past the police line. 'The moment his feet touched Danish soil a thousand people surged round the explorer, and the Crown Prince and those who accompanied him were wedged tightly in the mass of hero-worshippers,' the *Daily Telegraph & Courier* reported. 'The motor of the Crown Prince was overturned in the press, and Dr Cook and those with him were driven further and further in the opposite direction from that in which they desired to go.'[8]

It was a tumultuous return to civilisation. 'About me was a babel of sound, of which I heard, the whole time, no intelligible word,' Cook wrote. 'On both sides the press of people closed upon us. I fought like a swimmer, struggling for life, and, becoming helpless, was pushed and carried along. I walked two steps on the ground and five in the air ... I was weak and almost stifled. On both sides of me rushed a flood of blurred human faces. I was in a delirium.'[9]

The British journalist W.T. Stead was one of four people who formed a circle around Cook to protect him from the crush. 'Seeing that he was ill-prepared for a scrimmage,' Stead wrote, 'I flung my arms round him under the armpits and pressing backwards with all my weight I somewhat eased the pressure from behind. In front the solitary constable fought his way like a Trojan, followed closely by Minister Egan; behind him came Dr Cook. Another journalist, Mr [Frederic] Wile [of the *Daily Mail*] ... came to our help, and the four of us, surrounding the human centre of the press, struggled, staggering, swaying hither and thither amid the cheering, excited throng. Dr Cook had to give up his flowers, one of his cuffs was torn off and carried away as a trophy [Wile would keep it as a souvenir]; once or twice it seemed as if we should be carried off our feet.'[10]

Finally, they found themselves outside Copenhagen's Meteorological Institute and decided to seek refuge there. As the crowd continued to push forward, they feared they might be crushed against its gate, but the gate opened and they were able to get inside and draw breath. But Cook's reprieve was short-lived, as the crowd outside clamoured for him to reappear and Crown Prince Christian, arriving at the Institute shortly after Cook, asked him to go outside to speak to them.

'But I speak no Danish,' Cook said. 'They couldn't understand me, even if I had something to say, which I have not.'

'Speak anything in any language,' said Crown Prince Christian. 'They probably will not know the difference anyway.'[11]

So Cook went out onto the balcony to address the hundreds of people packed into the street below.

'My friends, I have had too hard a time getting here to make a speech,' he shouted. 'I can only say that I consider it an honour to be able to put my foot first on Danish soil.'[12]

Cook would later remember this impromptu speech, like much of his welcome in Copenhagen, as little more than a blur. 'I remember opening my mouth, but I do not know a word I said,' he wrote. 'There followed a lot of noise. I suppose it was applause. Emerging from the black, lonely Arctic night, the contrast of that rushing flood of human faces staggered me. Yes, there was another sensation – that of being a stranger among strange people, in a city where, however much I might be honoured, I had no old-time friend. This curiously depressed me.'[13]

While Cook struggled to adjust to the crowd's adulation, the *Hans Egede* had arrived at the quay and Gibbs left the ship and became caught in the crush. As he pushed his way through the sea of bodies, he saw his best friend in journalism, the *Daily Express*'s Alphonse Courlander, on the edge of the crowd. He excitedly shouted to him that he had spent two hours with Cook that morning, and Courlander looked at him hopefully, silently pleading for him to share some of the details. 'This was one of the few times when I played a lone hand, and I ran from him, and jumped on a taxi in order to avoid the call of comradeship,' Gibbs wrote. 'I knew I had the story of the world.'[14]

As Gibbs looked for somewhere to write his article, Cook was smuggled out of the back of the Meteorological Institute and into a carriage with the Danish explorer Andreas Hovgaard, who 30 years earlier had been part of the first expedition to make it through the Northeast Passage between Europe and Asia. The carriage took them through the crowded streets to the Hotel Phoenix, where Cook was to be put up as a guest of the Royal Danish Geographical Society. Fittingly, it was the hotel where the two main characters stay in Jules Verne's *Journey to the Centre of the Earth*.

The hotel's hallway was decorated with flowers and American flags, and Cook was greeted with a reception hosted by Danish Minister of Commerce Johann Hansen and a committee of the Royal Danish Geographical Society. They opened a bottle of champagne and there were three cheers for Cook, and Hansen invited him to attend a banquet in his honour at the city hall that evening. Then after the reception, Cook was introduced to a tailor, barber, and dentist, who set to work on turning him from what the American Minister Maurice Egan called 'the Robinson Crusoe figure of the morning' into a smart-suited gentleman with neatly trimmed hair and a closely cropped moustache. Then Egan took him to lunch at the American Legation, where admirers lined the stairs and photographers tried to force their way into the dining room as they ate.

Cook was then taken to the royal palace, spending two hours talking to King Frederick, Queen Louise, and their three daughters, before returning to the Hotel Phoenix to find a group of 60 journalists waiting for him. They were led by W.T. Stead, who while he had been protecting Cook from the crowd that morning had managed to extract an agreement from him to meet the press later that day. The journalists led Cook into an empty banquet hall so they could ask him questions and scrutinise his claim to have reached the Pole, the *London Daily News* correspondent writing that there was 'something grotesque' in the way that 'here was a man whose greatness will live as long as the world lasts arraigned like a prisoner in the dock'.[15]

W.T. Stead is one of the towering figures in British journalism history, his thick beard, piercing eyes, and religious fervour making him reminiscent of a figure from the Old Testament. Today, he is revered by journalists as a hero for his campaigning approach and for his willingness to go to jail as part of his campaign for tougher laws on child prostitution. But the reality was more complex. By 1909, his reputation in Britain had been tarnished by the credulity with which he embraced spiritualism. And while his campaign on child prostitution did help change the law, the disturbing details of it — he arranged to buy a 13-year-old girl and had her drugged and subjected to an unnecessary medical examination — make his three-month jail sentence for it seem less like journalistic martyrdom and more a case of getting off lightly. But whatever doubts existed about his journalism, his stature was such that he was the obvious person to preside over the press conference.

He started by asking Cook if he was absolutely sure he had discovered the North Pole.[16]

'I think so,' said Cook.

'You have set your foot right on it?' asked Stead.

'Oh, I couldn't say that. I got to where there wasn't any longitude.'

Stead gave Cook a good-natured slap on the shoulder, trying to put him at ease as he prepared to ask a delicate question. 'Well, Dr Cook, now mind you, these are not my personal sentiments — I am a Cookite myself from the top of my head to the soles of my feet — but the world, we can readily foresee, is going to be divided into Cookites and anti-Cookites. For the benefit of the Cookites, then, will you say, first, that all your records are authentic, and, second, that you consider yourself a competent man to take down records?'

Cook agreed this was the case.

'But you did not set your foot upon the exact point of the Pole?' Stead asked.

'I doubt if anybody could do that. I got within the circle, I think. I went around it for two days making observations.'

'From where you stood, you could have fired a bullet over the exact point?'

'Yes, I should say so.'

'Now some details as to your journey up there, Doctor – your dash to the Pole?'

'It was simply that – a dash. We did not try to carry all the heavy instruments. Therefore, there is nothing so very scientific about the achievement.'

'You say "we" travelled ...'

'Myself and the two Eskimos.*'

'You can get these two men to testify that you have been to the Pole?'

'Yes. That is, they know where they went. They have no knowledge of latitude and longitude. They can testify in a general way to the number of days' travel they made from a certain point of departure ... I am in this work for the love of the work, gentlemen. And I have brought back just exactly the sort of records and proofs that every Arctic explorer brings back.'

Stead opened the floor to the other journalists, and they fired more questions at him. Had he planted the Stars and Stripes at the Pole? (He had.) Had he enjoyed eating fox? Was he a Christian? ('Just say in a general way that I am.') How could the world be sure his observations were real? ('Why should I sit down and invent observations? I did not do this thing for anything but sport and because I take a real interest in the problem. It would not do me any good to invent these things.') Cook also clarified some of the details in his *New York Herald* article. The temperature he had recorded had been -83 degrees Fahrenheit rather than Celsius, and he had not set foot on the 30,000 square miles of new land he had discovered; he had only seen it from a distance.

As the press conference drew to a close, it fell to Stead to sum up the journalists' collective view: 'Some believed in Dr Cook at first; all believe in him now.'[17] Stead's fellow journalists signalled their

---

* The Inuit were commonly called 'Eskimos' during this period. This book refers to them as Inuit, but the quotes that use 'Eskimo' have not been changed.

agreement by coming forward to shake hands with Cook and ask for his autograph.

'Dr Cook modestly met every inquiry with a directness and frankness that quickly won all of his hearers,' reported the United Press.[18] The *London Daily News*'s headline was 'Belief in Dr Cook's story grows stronger', and its correspondent wrote that 'there were hardly any of us … who were not convinced by the genuineness of his claim'.[19] 'As the result of half an hour's most searching cross-examination,' wrote the *Times* correspondent, 'I am glad to be able to say that he entirely satisfied me as to his good faith. Sitting within a yard of him in the presence of an intensely interested room-full of people, we took him through his printed story. The look on his face was calm and the sincere manner in which he answered awkward questions produced on all present a profound impression. A private talk which I had with him this morning tended further to strengthen my belief, which apparently is shared by all who have met him, that he is an upright and honest man.'[20]

But one journalist not at the press conference was Philip Gibbs, who at that moment was sitting at a desk in another hotel, writing his article about his interview with Cook.

After the press conference, Cook prepared for dinner and was then driven the mile to the city hall through streets lined with thousands of people standing in the pouring rain in the hope of getting a glimpse of him. When they reached the city hall, with its clock tower casting an imposing presence over the city centre, Cook was greeted with a reception near the entrance, and then a band played 'The Star-Spangled Banner' as the diners walked upstairs to take their seats. In the banquet hall, Minister of Commerce Johann Hansen escorted Cook to the chair of honour to loud cheering that the *New York Times* correspondent noticed 'caused him to colour deeply'. Once the 400 diners were seated, there was a series of speeches, the Mayor of Copenhagen telling them a new name had been enrolled in the list of great explorers, and Maurice Egan declaring his pride that a fellow American had planted a flag where no human had set foot before. Johann Hansen said he hoped Cook would now try for the South Pole and he raised his glass to 'our noble guest', before Andreas Hovgaard, the explorer who had shared Cook's carriage earlier in the day, praised Cook for the methods he had used.

Then it was Cook's turn, and he got to his feet to address the gathering. 'I thank you very much for the warm and eloquent words, but I am unable to express myself properly,' he said. 'It was a rather hard day for me, but I never enjoyed a day better. The Danes have taken no active part in polar explorations, but they have been of much importance as silent partners in almost all Arctic expeditions in recent years. The most important factors in my expedition were the Eskimo and the dog, and I cannot be too thankful to the Danes for their care of the Eskimo. Had I not met with the right Eskimos and the right dogs and the right provisions, I could never have reached the Pole. I owe much to the Danish nation for my success.'

Among the diners listening to him was Gibbs. He had arrived late because he had not had evening dress with him, and so had gone back to the café from the previous evening and paid the waiter there the equivalent of a shilling to lend him his. It had grease stains on the waistcoat and was so big that 'his trousers had a concertina effect when I put them on' and 'his sleeves reached half-way down my hands'.[21] Gibbs felt 'like Hop-o'-my-Thumb in the giant's clothes' as he had to hold up his trousers as he climbed the steps to the banquet.[22]

The Frederick Cook who Gibbs saw at the banquet seemed almost a different man to the one he had met that morning. 'The shaggy explorer had disappeared, and here was a spruce man of civilisation,' Gibbs wrote in his article for the *Daily Chronicle*. 'I liked the shaggy man best. This was too much like a Jewish stockbroker. I could see now that the man is of Jewish race, as it has been stated. This accounts for a powerful nose, but not for his blue eyes. He is full of inconsistencies like this.'

Given his intelligence and love of culture, Gibbs's casual use of antisemitic language is shocking.[23] Just as disturbing as Gibbs thinking it acceptable to write it was the *Daily Chronicle* thinking it acceptable to publish it. As well as antisemitic, it was wrong: Cook's father was a Lutheran and his mother a Catholic.

'Curiously enough, too, it seemed to me as he sat at the table that the man had something of the Eskimo about him,' Gibbs continued, 'a certain hardness of skin and a curious mouth which shuts like a trap. I noticed that all through dinner, which lasted several hours, he sat still smiling and saying nothing. At least, he only answered by a word or two his neighbours on either hand, the American Minister and the Minister of Commerce, though he seemed quite self-possessed. His eyes were watchful, again very watchful. Only one thing betrayed the man who has lived with Eskimos – his large red hands, and as I saw him helping himself to dainties from silver dishes I thought of him in a hole in the frozen snow, eating rotten seal, while above and around was the darkness and eternal silence of the Arctic regions.'

As Gibbs's fellow diners listened to the speeches and enjoyed being part of an historic event, they could hardly have guessed that the Englishman in the ill-fitting and dirty suit who sat among them had already sent an article back to London that would set forth a chain of events that would change the lives of both him and Cook forever.[24]

5

GOING RIGHT AFTER HIM

Philip Gibbs had arrived at an out-of-the-way hotel earlier that day knowing the article he was about to write was by far the most important of his career so far.

The most obvious way to approach it would have been to simply report what Cook had told him and describe what it had been like to stand near him as they had approached the quay. But there was something about Cook that sat uneasily with Gibbs, and the more he replayed their conversation in his mind, the more he became convinced there were things about it that did not add up.

While Gibbs's first impression of Cook was of a 'typical sea-rover' with 'an honest face', as they had sat together in the dining saloon he had begun to detect something else: a sense of evasiveness and calculation that seemed at odds with that first impression. 'I began to be a little disappointed with those blue eyes,' Gibbs wrote. 'I could not fix them. They would not look into mine. I could not look through those windows into the man's soul. They were shy eyes avoiding a straight gaze, and they were restless eyes and watchful – very watchful. It seemed to me … that Dr Cook is always watching quietly to see what the world thinks of him. And while he watched he smiles, with a curious, shy, self-conscious smile. He smiles when a man speaks to him for quite a long time before he answers. He seems to think a good deal, and to be cautious with words.'

And when they started talking about his journey, his doubts began to grow.

'What evidence can you bring to show that you actually reached the North Pole?' Gibbs had asked him.

'I bring the same proofs as every other explorer,' Cook said, with a sudden flash of anger. 'I bring my story. Do you doubt that? When Shackleton and Peary came home you believed what they told you. Why, then, should you disbelieve me?'

'I had believed him,' Gibbs later wrote. 'But at that strange, excited protest and some uneasy, almost guilty look about the man, I thought, "Hullo! What's wrong? This man protests too much."'

Cook went on to explain that he had taken a series of consecutive observations on his way to the North Pole, which would be sufficient to prove his claim.

'That is very good,' Gibbs said. 'Then doubtless you have these ready with you. You have not lost them?'

Cook explained that he did not have a diary with him because he had given his papers to a man called Harry Whitney to take to New York.

'When will he get there?' Gibbs asked.

'Next year,' said Cook.

'But surely you have brought your journal with you? The essential papers?'

'I have no papers.'

Gibbs thought it odd that Cook had allowed himself to be separated from the evidence he would need to support his claim. He suddenly found himself contemplating the shocking idea that Cook might be lying about having reached the Pole. Gibbs was further troubled when Cook said he had not brought back any geological specimens, and seemed unable to explain why his final dash to the Pole had taken just three months but his journey back had taken three times longer. Then, as they were finishing talking, Cook pointed to a newspaper on the table that had a photograph of him with a beard.

'That is a very old photograph. I have not worn a beard for 15 years.'

'Do you mean you shaved at the North Pole?' Gibbs asked.

'No, I cut off the hair with scissors or hacked it off,' said Cook, with a laugh. 'No Arctic explorers wear beards or moustaches, as icicles would cling to them.'

This seemed strange to Gibbs, who thought he remembered photographs of polar explorers with full beards. Perhaps unaware that Cook had spent winters in both the Arctic and Antarctica, Gibbs began to suspect that he did not know as much about living in freezing conditions as he claimed, and this added to his accumulating doubts. He would later remember that 'by intuition, rather than evidence, by some quick instinct of facial expression, by some sensibility to mental and moral dishonesty, I was convinced, absolutely, at the end of an hour, that this man had not been to the North Pole, but was attempting to bluff the world'.[1]

The moment he made up his mind was when Carl Martin Norman Hansen asked Cook to come onto the deck as they approached the quay, and Cook seemed to hesitate and had to be persuaded to come out. 'Cook was green,' Gibbs wrote. 'He looked like a criminal who had lost his nerve and knows that discovery is inevitable. The little devil doubt was growing big in my brain.'[2] Then, later, Gibbs saw Peter Freuchen, who had somehow managed to get onto the *Hans Egede* and was standing at the back when Cook talked to Gibbs and the two Danish journalists, and he asked him what he made of Cook's story. Freuchen replied noncommittally that he was not in a position to judge.

'But I thought you had been up to the Arctic?' Gibbs said. 'You must know something about it.'

Freuchen paused, apparently hesitant to say what he really thought. 'Yes, and I have a hunch his whole story is a damned lie,' he said finally.

Gibbs nodded. 'I thought Cook was a faker from the first, and now I'm going right after him,' he said.[3]

So as Gibbs began to write his article, he did not want to join in the praise of someone he now believed to be lying. Yet he had no firm evidence, and if he were to accuse Cook of fraud and Cook was later shown to be telling the truth, his reputation would be ruined and the *Daily Chronicle* would be exposed to an expensive libel action. So Gibbs split the difference, writing an article that did not go as far as to accuse Cook of lying, but which focused so intently on his answers to difficult questions that it was obvious Gibbs thought his claim should not be taken at face value. Gibbs reinforced this impression by including lines such as, 'Surely he should have retained the strongest proofs of his claim so that it might be immediately established', and, 'Whether his answers seem satisfactory, I will leave my readers to judge'.

Gibbs had not been at the press conference, but in his article he claimed Cook's answers to Stead's questions had 'caused a great deal of uneasiness', contradicting the accounts of the journalists who were actually there. And Gibbs again revealed his own prejudice when he told of his surprise at Cook saying the Inuit were 'an intelligent and cultured people', because Gibbs 'had always thought the Eskimos were the most primitive and ignorant race on earth'.

'All through my account there was the strong suggestion of doubt as to the truth of his claim,' Gibbs later wrote. 'I did not call him a liar and a charlatan, but every reader would know that I disbelieved him. I took a big chance, and looking back on it one which was too dangerous and not quite justified. I had no proof whatever that he was a fraud.'[4] He admitted just how big a risk he was taking: 'The whole of it amounted to a case of libel. When I handed it into the telegraph office I knew I had burned my boats, and that my whole journalistic career would be made or marred by this message ... I will not disguise my sense of anxiety. I had a deep conviction that my judgement was right, but whether I should be able to maintain my position by direct evidence was not so certain in my mind.'[5]

6

THIS BAFFLING MAN

The next day was a Sunday, the only day of the week when the *Daily Chronicle* did not publish an edition. So Gibbs's article appeared instead on the front pages of *Lloyd's Weekly Newspaper* in Britain and *The New York Times*, both of which had news-sharing agreements with the *Chronicle*.

Both newspapers presented his article in a way that reinforced Gibbs's doubts. *Lloyd's Weekly Newspaper* highlighted the quote 'You believed Peary: Why not me?', and *The New York Times* chose the headline, 'Cook under fire sticks to story'.[1] After three days of mostly celebratory newspaper coverage, Gibbs's reporting landed like a bombshell in London and New York, and news of it quickly reached Copenhagen and caused what Gibbs called an 'immense sensation'.

The Denmark of September 1909 was a country that was divided and uncertain about the direction it should be taking. It had spent the summer gripped by a political crisis after the government resigned because it could not get its defence budget through parliament, with widespread anxiety about the extent to which Denmark should prepare to defend itself in an increasingly dangerous world. Cook's arrival was a welcome distraction. The Danes were proud that he had chosen Copenhagen for his return to civilisation, and Cook seemed a hero the whole country could unite behind. American Minister Maurice Egan later wrote that 'the coming of Dr Cook was a godsend to the Danish government [and] … made such a diversion that the question between the Moderates and the Socialists … was almost forgotten'.[2] So by openly questioning Cook's story, Gibbs suddenly found himself transformed from an anonymous journalist into one of the most talked about people in Copenhagen, a ghost at the feast who threatened to cast a pall over one of the greatest celebrations in its history. In the days that followed, he would be personally criticised by Denmark's newspapers and even booed by his fellow diners in a restaurant.

This hostility was difficult for someone as shy and sensitive as Gibbs, and he also felt the pressure of knowing his credibility was now on the line. So having gone public with his intuition that Cook was lying, Gibbs now set out to try to prove it.

He started by looking for experts on polar exploration, hoping they might be able to spot any discrepancies in Cook's account. The first person he chose was the legendary Norwegian explorer Otto Sverdrup, who along with the explorer Fridtjof Nansen had been one of the first people to cross Greenland, had been part of Nansen's 'farthest north' expedition of 1895, and had himself mapped many hundreds of miles of Arctic coast. Cook had credited Sverdrup's discoveries with giving him the idea for his route to the Pole, and Gibbs had heard that Cook was claiming Sverdrup had vouched for his truthfulness. He wanted to hear for himself what Sverdrup thought of his claim, and arranged to meet him for lunch.

As they shook hands, Gibbs thought the 54-year-old Sverdrup seemed a 'splendid-looking man, with a big golden beard like one of the old Danish Vikings', and was impressed by his 'grand simplicity of manner'.[3] Gibbs started by asking him if he had seen Cook since he had arrived in Copenhagen.

'Yes, I had a few minutes' conversation with him. He seemed glad to see me, saying that the plans in my last book had taught him to reach the Pole.'

Gibbs asked Sverdrup if he believed Cook had really reached the Pole. Sverdrup paused, looking at Gibbs and shaking his beard as he thought. 'I have no reason to doubt his story,' he said, finally. 'He says he has found the North Pole, and I am bound to believe him.'

'But did he give you any proof?'

'No.'

'Did he show you any of his observations?'

'No.'

'Did he show you any of his photographs?'

'No, sir.'

'Did you have an opportunity of questioning him as to the details?'

'No. He was surrounded by people all wanting to talk to him, and I was only with him a short time.'

'Did he look you straight in the eyes as you are looking at me?'

'No, but some people are different from others.'

'Did he show you any of his maps?'

'No, but he pointed to a map of the Arctic regions published in a newspaper and showed me where he discovered new land.'

'Therefore you have no more facts than the rest of us?'

'Nothing but his simple statement, that is all,' said Sverdrup. 'It is certainly a pity that he did not have another white man with him.'

But Sverdrup was at least able to reassure Gibbs that the 15 miles a day Cook claimed to have travelled over broken ice was entirely possible, as Sverdrup had himself sometimes travelled 25 miles in a day on his last expedition.

Gibbs thanked Sverdrup for his time, disappointed not to have uncovered any holes in Cook's story, but relieved that at least Sverdrup's endorsement of him fell short of what he had been told. He then went to see Andreas Hovgaard, who at the previous evening's banquet had been full of praise for Cook's methods of exploration. Gibbs introduced himself, asking the explorer the same question he had asked Sverdrup: did he believe Cook had reached the Pole?

'That can never be proved,' said Hovgaard. 'One must only accept his word.'

'But surely if, as he says, he has kept a record of his observations, they will afford absolute proof one way or the other?'

'No, certainly not. There is nothing to prevent imaginary observations being written down. I could invent any number of them with the greatest ease in my own study.'

'How about the flag which Dr Cook says he left at the North Pole?'

'That will afford no proof whatever, because it will never be found again at the Pole even if it is there now. Dr Cook himself says there is no land at the Pole, and if he stuck it in the ice it will be carried goodness knows how many miles southward.'[4]

Gibbs thanked Hovgaard for his time and left him to return to his hotel to write an article about the two interviews for the next day's *Daily Chronicle*. As with his article the previous day, he wrote it in a way that focused so intently on the question of whether Cook really had reached the Pole that it implied there was good reason to doubt him.

While Gibbs was trying to build the case against him, Cook continued to receive congratulations from all over the world, including a telegram from US President William Taft. 'Your report that you have reached the North Pole,' wrote Taft, 'calls for my heartiest congratulations and stirs the pride of all Americans that this feat, which has so long baffled the world, has been accomplished by the intelligent energy and the wonderful endurance of a fellow-countryman.'

That afternoon, Cook visited the American Legation, spending time with Professor Elis Strömgren, the head of Copenhagen's Astronomical Observatory who was so distinguished that he would be nominated for Nobel prizes and have an asteroid named after him, and Professor Carl Torp, the rector of the University of Copenhagen. They asked him detailed questions about his expedition as a kind of due diligence before deciding whether to recommend him for formal honours. Then, that evening, Cook dined with King Frederick and his family at the summer palace, and during dinner Cook was seated next to the king, an honour no one could remember being given to a private individual.[5] After the other guests left, the king and queen gave Cook what newspapers called the 'most unusual honour' of asking him and Maurice Egan to stay and take tea with the royal family alone.[6]

The following morning, Monday, 6 September, the *Daily Chronicle* printed Gibbs's article about his interviews with Sverdrup and Hovgaard, along with his article about the banquet on the Saturday night. In reporting Cook's speech at the banquet, Gibbs made his distrust for him even clearer:

At last I thought he will show us into the heart of this mystery and say, 'In this way, and by this means, did I reach the North Pole,' but, no, it was another opportunity lost. This baffling man still kept his secret, and in returning thanks for the welcome given to him did not give us any facts by which his claim could be tested, did not indeed give us any facts at all, but only a few phrases of conversational thanks … Dr Cook has now been in Copenhagen two days, and has had plenty of time, therefore, to convince the world of the truth of his claim that he reached the North Pole. Has he convinced the world? I do not know. But certainly in Copenhagen, where there are many men familiar with Arctic exploration, there are many also who are filled with a sense of uneasiness.

In two days Dr Cook has been given many opportunities of producing his proofs, but he has not yet used those opportunities … No doubt Dr Cook has been overwhelmed by his reception, and certainly in lunching and dining with the Royalty and Ministers of Denmark he has been kept busy. But still the world waits for only one thing – his proof. That has not yet been given. It is strange and charming to find some of the people here with such faith in human nature that they are willing to believe without it, waiting in confidence for it to come. I, at least, as one of the reporters of the world's history, must, in duty to the public, be sceptical until the facts are proven, without, however, denying the truth of Dr Cook's story.

As well as publishing Gibbs's article, the *Daily Chronicle* weighed in with questions of its own. Apparently determined to make up for its slow start in covering the story, its news editor Ernest Perris had been busy assembling a group of polar experts to advise them on it. This meant the *Chronicle* was now able to open new lines of attack in an editorial headlined 'Grave discrepancies'.

It noted that Cook's account was 'peculiarly lacking in plain records of fact', and described his decision to send his books straight to America as displaying 'an ingenuousness almost beyond belief'. It thought it was 'incredible that Dr Cook should have parted with a shred of the testimony which must form his credentials to the scientific societies of Europe', given that in the cases of other polar explorers 'these records have been clung to and preserved when almost everything else has been abandoned'. Did it make sense, the *Chronicle* asked, for Cook to have left his records in Greenland in the hope that someone would carry them to America after he had left? Or if he had put them on a boat to America himself, why had he not gone to America with them, given their preciousness and the fact that a boat to America would have offered the chance of a reunion with the wife he had not seen for two years?

And while Sverdrup may have thought travelling 15 miles in a day was unexceptional, the *Chronicle* thought it unlikely Cook could have travelled so quickly given the poor quality of the ice he had described in his account of his expedition. The *Chronicle* also thought his observations of the sun were too exact to be credible, and questioned his claim to have used an artificial horizon (an instrument for measuring altitude) because the mercury in it would have frozen at the temperatures he said he had recorded. It also doubted his claim to have seen purple snow, arguing that this only occurs when ice has land beneath it, and Cook had said there was no land at the Pole. Like Gibbs, the *Chronicle* did not openly accuse Cook of lying, but made clear that it thought the fact he had not already produced proof of his achievement raised serious questions. 'Dr Cook has now for more than 24 hours had an opportunity of submitting his proofs to Europe and the world,' it concluded. 'At best he has done no more than repeat the statements he has already made. But in some important particulars he has either qualified or withdrawn his original utterances. In that connection it need only be noted that Dr Cook's description of his travels confided to the *New York Herald* was not a slapdash dispatch, but a considered narrative, of which he must have pondered for months. If the facts and figures which he then put forward will not withstand the first shock of criticism, it is scarcely likely that the rest of the story is to be depended upon.'

For one of Britain's leading newspapers to openly question Cook's honesty was a startling new development in the story. But for now, at least, most journalists in Copenhagen were prepared to continue giving him the benefit of the doubt. 'The air is thick with assertions equally positive and contradictory, and the task of forming a sane opinion is more than usually embarrassing,' the *Times* correspondent admitted. 'It is impossible to deny that Dr Cook's account of his journey still presents a large number of points requiring explanation. It is more likely that, pestered to death as he is at all hours of the day and night, so short a time after his return to civilization, a man of his type of intellectual capacity may make statements which appear to conflict with others made under different conditions. The fact remains that he is here and continues to produce upon those who talk to him a strong impression of his good faith.'[7]

7

THE GRAVEST SUSPICION

When he woke on Monday, 6 September, Gibbs would have been expecting to spend the day continuing to build his case against Cook. Instead, he suddenly found himself forced onto the defensive. A journalist told him that when Cook had talked to Professors Strömgren and Torp at the American Legation the previous day, he had apparently shown them observations he had recorded at the Pole, and Strömgren had been so impressed that he had confirmed his belief in Cook to a group of journalists waiting outside. 'Gentlemen, I am perfectly satisfied, having studied Dr Cook's diary with his daily record of observations, that there is no reason for any shadow of doubt as to the fact that he reached the Pole,' he had reportedly told them.

This was at odds with what Cook himself had told Gibbs about having sent his observations to America. But if he really had shown Strömgren observations and Strömgren had been convinced by them, Gibbs's case would be fatally undermined. And this was more than just a rumour – that day, the *Daily Mail* correspondent sent an article to London reporting that Strömgren and Torp had been so impressed by Cook that the Royal Danish Geographical Society was planning to present him its prestigious gold medal and the University of Copenhagen had decided to award him an honorary degree.[1]

'I was ready to telegraph the great news and to say there need be no more doubt that Dr Cook is the hero of the North Pole,' Gibbs wrote in his report for the next day's *Chronicle*. 'I was ready to take off my hat to Dr Cook, although this flatly contradicted his words to me that he had sent his books to America for some extraordinary reason from Greenland.' But whatever Gibbs may have said publicly, the news must have felt like a hammer blow for a man who, having staked his reputation on his belief that Cook was lying, now seemed to have lost. It must have been one of the times Gibbs would later look back on as 'moments when I had frightful doubts about the line I was taking' and worried that 'I was maligning an honest and heroic man'.

That morning, he saw W.T. Stead, who maintained what Gibbs called a 'sunny and sturdy belief' in Cook.

'Is it true, then, that Dr Cook brought his diary with him and submitted his observations to the Astronomical Institute?' Gibbs asked him.

'Yes,' said Stead. 'He told me that himself.'

'Then why did he tell me that he had sent his books to America by way of Greenland?'

'Well, I don't exactly understand that, but he told me that he had sent his rough manuscripts to America and had brought his diary and principal records here. But why doubt the man? He is a simple, honest fellow. At least, as I told him to his face, he is either a simple honest fellow or an imposter, and that I don't believe. I am for Cook, heart and soul.'

Stead told Gibbs he had also heard that Otto Sverdrup had seen a sealed black bag that Cook had with him that apparently contained his observations, though Stead added that 'I am not quite sure whether he actually saw the documents'.

'Well, Mr Stead, I am very glad to hear what you tell me,' Gibbs said. 'My doubts are all but gone. If Dr Cook has shown his observations to the Astronomical Society and they are satisfied, it is all settled.'

Anxious to know for sure, Gibbs went straight to see Strömgren at the Copenhagen University Observatory.

'Professor, I understand that you have seen Dr Cook's manuscripts,' he said, after introducing himself and presenting Strömgren with his card.

'What manuscripts?' asked Strömgren, looking surprised.

'His diary.'

'His diary I have not seen.'

'But surely, did you not examine his observations?'

'No, I have seen no observations. He showed me only a paper on which he had written the results of his journey.'

'Were they scientifically accurate?'

'They were scientifically valueless. They were not observations at all. They were merely statements. They could prove neither one thing nor the other. Until we can see his original observations, we can prove nothing at all. It is impossible to examine any observations made by Dr Cook. There are no original observations in Copenhagen. Dr Cook told me himself that he had sent them all to America from Greenland. He has nothing with him here, he says, but his results.'

This contradicted what Gibbs had been told. He asked Strömgren to repeat what he had said and Strömgren did so, slowly and deliberately, his expression grave.

'Then there is no diary here?' said Gibbs, checking again.

'No, there is no diary in Copenhagen.'

'And therefore no proof whatever that Dr Cook's story is true?'

'That is so.'

In his article about his interview with Strömgren, Gibbs wrote that he left the observatory with 'troubled thoughts' because this seemed 'very serious for Dr Cook'. But he is more likely to have left with a spring in his step. The threat of imminent reputational ruin had lifted, and the fact that Cook seemed to have wrongly claimed to have shown his observations to Strömgren appeared to be more evidence against him. Gibbs then went from the observatory to see Otto Sverdrup, asking him about what Stead had heard about Cook showing him his papers. A bemused Sverdrup replied that he had not seen any papers. Again, it raised the question of how the rumour had started.

After finishing with Sverdrup, Gibbs met Dagmar Rasmussen and Peter Freuchen for lunch, and they were joined by the *Daily Chronicle*'s Copenhagen correspondent Oscar Hansen. Having already helped him get his interview with Cook, Gibbs hoped Dagmar Rasmussen would be able to give him new information, as over the last two days there had been lots of public discussion about Knud Rasmussen's views on Cook's claim. They were seen as important because the charismatic 30-year-old explorer and anthropologist was himself part Inuit, had been born and raised in Greenland, and was one of the world's leading experts on Inuit culture. He had also been one of the last people to see Cook before he set off for the Pole. Cook had apparently said that Knud Rasmussen had spoken to the Inuit who had accompanied him to the Pole, and the Danish Inspector of North Greenland had reportedly confirmed this and said the Inuit had corroborated Cook's story.

With Knud Rasmussen still in the north, Gibbs hoped Dagmar Rasmussen would be able to shed more light on her husband's views than had already appeared in the press. So when she pulled out a letter from her husband, Gibbs immediately realised its significance.

'You, of all men, would like to read that letter,' she said.

'Alas that I do not know Danish!'

She took out a pencil and marked a paragraph in the letter. 'Perhaps I will let you copy out those words.'

Gibbs tore a piece of paper from his notebook and handed it to Freuchen, who copied out the words in Danish and then on the same piece of paper Oscar Hansen translated them into English. As Hansen wrote, Gibbs felt a sense of rising excitement as he realised the extract was potentially devastating for Cook's claim and offered him the chance to go back on the offensive after a morning spent worrying about Strömgren and Sverdrup.

'My first impression when I heard about Dr Cook was an enormous disappointment, and I am sorry,' Knud Rasmussen had written. 'I have not spoken to the two Eskimos, who, according to Dr Cook, had followed him to the North Pole, but have only seen the 10 Eskimos who were sent back.'

The first sentence seemed a strange thing to write about someone who was supposed to be his friend. The second sentence seemed to contradict Cook's claim that Knud Rasmussen had spoken to the Inuit.

Dagmar Rasmussen gave Gibbs permission to publish the extract from the letter in the *Daily Chronicle*, and with lunch eaten he hurried off to write his article for the next day's edition. Emboldened by his interviews with Strömgren and Sverdrup and the extract from Knud Rasmussen's letter, he now felt confident enough to leave no doubt at all that he thought Cook was lying.

He wrote that the extract from the letter was 'absolutely a denial of Dr Cook's own words' and that it threw 'the gravest suspicion upon the word of honour of Dr Cook'. 'It is a remarkable thing,' he wrote, 'that in spite of his silence upon the most essential points, and in spite of the most contradictory statements when he has spoken, Dr Cook has steadily won over many people who were at first doubtful of his claim, yet they can give no reasons for their belief now beyond the impression made by his personality. That personality is so strange and so powerful that I believe if Cook claimed to have come from Mars there would be many people who would say, "We believe him because he tells us so. Such a simple, honest man would not deceive us." Dr Cook so far has produced no more evidence of a journey to the North Pole than he could show in reference to Mars. I do not say he will not produce it, but he has not done so yet.'[2]

Gibbs wrote that 'all my doubts have increased a thousand-fold' after the day's events, and his conclusion was all the more damning for the precision with which he chose his words: 'I will even say, with a full sense of my responsibility in using the words, that Dr Cook's honour and veracity are most seriously challenged.'

Gibbs's article was accompanied by another *Daily Chronicle* editorial. 'If the world is today divided into Cookites and Anti-Cookites, and there is a strong difference of opinion as to the righteousness of his claims, Dr Cook has only himself to thank,' it argued. 'If he finds himself, on his return to civilisation, in an atmosphere not so cordial as he could wish, it must be set down to the peculiar and unprecedented methods of exploration which he has followed. It cannot be said that he has met reasonable criticism in the best spirit.'

It went on to challenge Cook's claim that he had no incentive for lying about reaching the Pole because he had not been paid for the trip: 'What a man has to "gain" by discovering the North Pole must already be evident to Dr Cook. A leap from obscurity into universal fame is the first fruit, and the crop of glory to be reaped in the immediate future is superabundant. Looking at the thing from the lowest level, there have already been offers of £50,000 for a series of lectures; agents for a lighter form of entertainment are flocking to Copenhagen with blank cheques.'

Because any observations would need to be checked against the accuracy of the instruments used to record them, the *Chronicle* thought it would be impossible for Cook to prove his claim without his instruments. It also saw Cook's admission at the press conference that he may not have stood on the exact spot of the Pole as a 'very considerable modification' of what he had written in his *New York Herald* article, an article that, the *Chronicle* reminded its readers, was not 'a hasty message, written in white heat, on the spur of the moment', but 'the concentrated essence of long deliberation'.

'He has shown extraordinary enterprise and determination in his endeavour to pierce the secrets of the unknown,' it concluded. 'He may or may not have succeeded. All that can be said at present, in the absence of definite evidence – most of which appears to be on its way to America – is that when Dr Cook thought he was at the North Pole he may, perhaps, have been no nearer it than Lieutenant Shackleton was to the South Pole nine months later. The difference is that Lieutenant Shackleton knew.'

As Gibbs and the *Chronicle*'s leader writer finished their articles for the next day's edition, they would have reasonably thought that the increasingly accusatory tone of their articles would further increase the pressure on Cook. But by the time they were published, they would be completely eclipsed by a twist in the story so extraordinary as to be scarcely believable.

Now that the story of Cook's arrival in Denmark had been written, the world's journalists were preparing to leave Copenhagen and the *Politiken* newspaper hosted a farewell dinner for the foreign press in the banquet room of the Tivoli Casino. Explorers Carl Martin Norman Hansen and Otto Sverdrup were also there, and while Cook initially declined his invitation, some reporters went to the Hotel Phoenix and persuaded him to come. Gibbs and W.T. Stead were among the 16 journalists in dress suits who loudly clapped Cook's entrance, holding glasses of schnaps as they sang 'He's a Jolly Good Fellow' and then raising glasses of champagne to toast the pronouncement that 'Dr Cook's name will shine like a star for generations to come' (whether Gibbs joined in with the applause and the singing is not recorded). The journalists were given gifts of Arctic-related porcelain animals from the Royal Porcelain Factory that *Politiken* had commissioned as mementos of their time in Copenhagen. A garland of flowers was then wrapped around Cook's shoulders, and the journalists again warmly applauded the man who had given them one of the biggest stories of their lives.[3]

The party was in full swing and the journalists were listening to a talk by a representative of the French newspaper *Le Matin*, when a messenger came in and handed an envelope to *Politiken*'s publisher. The publisher opened it, looked surprised, and then passed it to W.T. Stead. Stead rose from his seat and raised his hand to ask for quiet. He then announced that he had just been given a telegram that had been sent to the Associated Press from Labrador in north-east Canada and proceeded to read it to them: 'Stars and Stripes nailed to North Pole. Peary.'

Mankind had dreamed of reaching the North Pole for hundreds of years, and for hundreds of years the North Pole had resisted every effort to discover its secrets. The many men who had risked their lives in pursuit of it were all united by the fact that every single one of them had failed. Now, after a long succession of heroic failures, two men had come forward within a matter for days to say they had succeeded.

8

REALM OF FAIRY TALES

It is difficult to imagine a polar explorer more different to Frederick Cook than Robert Peary. An imposing figure with a large moustache and hard blue eyes, the writer Fergus Fleming has described Peary as 'undoubtedly the most driven, possibly the most successful, and probably the most unpleasant man in the annals of polar exploration'.[1] While Cook's modesty and affability endeared him to most people he met, the author John Edward Weems has written of how Peary 'radiated superiority through his commanding manner and his impressive physique, thus antagonising many persons at first meeting'.[2]

While Cook's Arctic career had given him a deep respect for the Inuit, Peary was capable of treating them with a callousness that was shocking even in 1909. He had two children with an Inuit despite himself being married. After becoming the first American to reach the Cape York meteorite in Greenland, he had it shipped back to the United States and sold it for $50,000, despite its great importance to the local community. He dug up Inuit graves and sold the bodies to the American Museum of Natural History as anthropological specimens, and convinced six Inuit to come back with him with promises of warm homes and better lives. He then abandoned them to be kept in the museum basement; within months, four of them were dead.

Peary also had a reputation among his fellow explorers as a prickly, domineering character, with a history of falling out with people.

He once wrote to his mother that 'I must be the peer or superior of those about me to be comfortable',[3] and there was a suspicion that the reason he recruited relatively inexperienced men to his expeditions was because they would feel less able to challenge him. He also tended to view Greenland, and the North Pole, in particular, as his own domain, which meant he often butted up against other explorers. He angrily dismissed Fridtjof Nansen's first crossing of Greenland as the 'forestalling of my work', and when Otto Sverdrup arrived in the Arctic while he was there in 1898, he accused the Norwegian of 'appropriation'. In fact, he became so fixated with the idea of not being beaten by Sverdrup (despite there being no suggestion that Sverdrup intended to compete with him) that he embarked on a near-suicidal journey that resulted in the loss of several of his toes.[4] So it was unsurprising that his reaction to the news that Cook was planning to attempt to reach the Pole had been one of fury; he wrote to *The New York Times* to complain that 'he is appropriating to his own use the services of the Eskimos whom I have trained', and that 'I regard Dr Cook's action in going north ... for the admitted purpose of forestalling me as one of which no man possessing a sense of honour would be guilty'.[5]

But whatever Peary's failings as a person, there was no doubting the 53-year-old's formidable reputation as an explorer. He had dreamed of the North Pole for decades, and had built up an astonishing record of achievement over a career he once described as '23 years of effort, hard work, disappointments, hardships, privations, more or less suffering, and some risks'.[6] On his first Arctic expedition in 1886 he reached further inland of the ice cap of Greenland than anyone before him, and then in 1891 returned from Greenland to announce he had proved it was an island (this was the expedition Cook was part of).

Three years later, he reached the Cape York meteorite, and then returned to the Arctic between 1898 and 1902, leading three failed attempts to reach the North Pole (it was after his second attempt that Cook had visited him and given him a medical examination). He tried yet again in 1906, not managing to reach the Pole but returning with the news that he had broken the 'farthest north' record by getting 36 miles closer to it than Umberto Cagni had six years earlier, and that he had also discovered a vast new land that he called Crocker Land after George Crocker, an American banker who had given him financial backing. His achievement was recognised at a National Geographic Society banquet (the same one Cook was a guest of honour at for having climbed McKinley), US President Theodore Roosevelt presenting him with a special gold medal and telling him 'you did a great deed, a deed that counted for all mankind, a deed which reflected credit upon you and upon your country'.[7] Then in 1908, spurred on by the news that Cook was attempting to claim a prize he thought should be his, Peary set off again on what was, given his age and failing health, probably his last chance to reach the North Pole.

He had not been heard from for some time, but now his telegram from many hundreds of miles away created an electrifying effect on Cook's celebratory dinner in Copenhagen. The journalists animatedly debated whether it was a hoax and, deciding it was probably real, reached for their notebooks and watched Cook closely for his reaction, the *Daily Mail* correspondent Frederic Wile writing that 'we naturally burned with curiosity to see whether and how Cook would stand the shock'.[8]

But if they expected him to be ruffled by the news, they were wrong. He responded in the same way he had responded to everything since arriving in Copenhagen – with apparent calmness and generosity of spirit.

'I am proud that a fellow American has reached the Pole,' he told the journalists. 'As Rear Admiral [Winfield Scott] Schley said at Santiago [during the Spanish–American war], "There is glory enough for all of us." He is a brave man, and I am confident that if the reports are true his observations will confirm mine and set at rest all doubts.'

The hosts of the dinner attempted to carry on with the meal, but everyone's attention was now elsewhere. One newspaper reported that the speeches 'were fewer than had been expected, and were notably listless', and 'only the personality of Dr Cook kept the banquet from disintegration'.[9] Before long, journalists began to slip away to send messages back to their newspapers in time for the next day's editions. Cook finished his dinner and afterwards chatted to Otto Sverdrup in what *The New York Times* called a 'most unconcerned manner'. Then, with the garland of roses still around his neck, he was led through the casino to a waiting car, where hundreds of people were gathered behind a police cordon to cheer him as he was driven away.[10]

The next day's newspapers reported Peary's claim as breathlessly as they had Cook's six days earlier, their articles filled with exhilaration at how the sudden emergence of a second North Pole claimant had created a sense of human drama unprecedented in the history of polar exploration.

Alongside their articles about Peary, the *Daily Chronicle* and *The New York Times* printed Gibbs's report about his interviews with Strömgren and Sverdrup and the extract from Knud Rasmussen's letter. But as well as his article being overshadowed by Peary's telegram, by the time it appeared it had already been undermined by a statement that University Rector Carl Torp had given to the *Daily Mail* about his meeting with Cook the previous Sunday.[11]

'I may say that Dr Cook stood the test perfectly, although the examination was of an intricate and scientific character,' said Professor Torp. 'There was not a detail or question put before him to which he failed to reply in the most satisfactory way. As there were certain questions of a special astronomical nature with which I myself was not sufficiently acquainted, I called in our greatest astronomical scientist, Professor Strömgren, who put an exhaustive series of mathematical and technical and natural and scientific questions to Dr Cook, based particularly on those of his contentions on which some doubts have been cast. Dr Cook answered them all to our full satisfaction. He showed no nervousness or excitement at any time. I dare say, therefore, there is no justification for anybody to throw the slightest doubt on his claim to have reached the North Pole and the means whereby he did it. Professor Strömgren and I were entirely satisfied with the evidence laid before us.'

Torp's statement was effectively a denial of what Strömgren had told Gibbs – that Cook's lack of evidence meant the question of whether he had reached the Pole was purely one of whether his word was to be believed. The *Daily Chronicle* office telegraphed the quote to Gibbs along with two words: 'Please explain.'

For the second time in two days, Gibbs's belief that Cook was lying seemed to have been shown to be wrong, but this time the stakes were even higher because of Gibbs's claim in his latest article that Cook's 'honour and veracity are most seriously challenged'. This time, Gibbs did not even try to pretend he would be pleased if Cook was shown to be telling the truth. 'I was thunderstruck and dismayed, for if the Rector ... maintained a belief in the bona fides of Cook, I was utterly undone,' he wrote.

When W.T. Stead saw Gibbs that morning, he was grave-faced and put his hand on his shoulder.

'Young man,' he said solemnly, 'you have not only ruined yourself, which does not matter very much, but you have also ruined the *Daily Chronicle*, for which I have had a great esteem.'

Gibbs pleaded with Stead for help. 'Mr Stead, I am a young and obscure man compared with you, and I appeal to your chivalry. Will you come with me to Strömgren, and act as my witness to the questions I shall put to him, and to the answers he gives?'[12]

'By all means,' said Stead. 'And to make things beyond doubt we will take two other witnesses.'[13]

So that afternoon, Gibbs, Stead and two other journalists went to see Strömgren. It was a tense meeting, and Strömgren at first refused to say anything at all about Cook. But Stead set forth with an eloquent exposition of how Gibbs's honour was at stake, and so it was only right that Strömgren should tell them what he knew. Finally, Strömgren seemed ready to talk.

Gibbs started by asking Strömgren if he had seen any of Cook's manuscripts. He paused for a long time while he considered his answer.

'No,' he said, at last.

Had he seen Cook's diary or journal?

'No.'

Had he seen any of Cook's original observations?

'No.'

'Did Cook tell you that he had no original observations in Copenhagen?'

'Yes.'

'Did you tell me that without such observations proof was impossible to obtain?'

Strömgren looked uncomfortable as he thought about the question. The four journalists watched him as the seconds ticked past. Then, finally, the answer came: 'Yes.'

Gibbs sighed with relief. As Strömgren seemed to have been put under pressure not to question Cook's claim, Gibbs wrote out a statement for him to sign: 'At the wish of Mr Gibbs, *Daily Chronicle*, I state that I have not seen the records of observations of Dr Cook. My impression of the trustworthiness of Cook's claim rests on a verbal conversation about his observations, which was satisfying to me.'

Strömgren said he did not want to sign it, but Gibbs pleaded with him and he reluctantly agreed. But after he signed it and handed it back to Gibbs, he added: 'Of course, that must not be published in the newspapers.'

Gibbs began to lose his temper, telling Strömgren it was worthless unless he could publish it. Stead and one of the other journalists agreed, arguing that the accuracy of Gibbs's report was being called into question, and so it was only right that Strömgren's statement should be published to make the position clear. Finally, Strömgren conceded, and Gibbs thanked him and hurried out of the room, anxious to get away before he changed his mind. He went back to his hotel to write an article about the encounter that bristled with anger at Torp and Strömgren's willingness to accept Cook's story without proof.

'It has been published to the world,' Gibbs wrote, 'that Professor Strömgren and Professor Torp examined Dr Cook exhaustively, mathematically, technically, and scientifically for two hours, and were entirely satisfied, especially upon points upon which doubt had been cast. I say that that statement is untrue. I have proved absolutely that that is untrue. And in proving it I prove also that all these honours being given to Cook are not justified on the facts; that the King of Denmark has been deceived, and that the whole world believes there is proof when there is no proof. I did not ask the Professor how his faith in Dr Cook could be reconciled by his statement that, without the original observations, there could be no proof. But I leave this to my readers, who will also observe that the representative of science in Denmark is willing to believe, without proof, as the King and the American Ambassador and all others have been persuaded.'

The same day, Gibbs met up with Peter Freuchen. Freuchen had been involved in the Cook story even before Gibbs arrived in Copenhagen, as the *Politiken* newspaper had enlisted the 23-year-old to help with its coverage because they thought his knowledge of the Arctic would be useful. But his journalistic career had got off to an embarrassing start when he told a *Politiken* journalist that Cook had reached the Pole on the day of the Spring Equinox, and so would have been there when the sun shot its rays across the ice for the first time that year. This resulted in *Politiken* publishing a poetic description of Cook's triumph, but the equinox had actually been the previous month and Freuchen was left feeling 'sick about it' after rival newspapers gleefully pointed out the error. Then, following Cook's arrival, he wrote an article setting out why he thought Cook was lying, but *Politiken*'s editor refused to publish it, telling him that 'we cannot wine and dine a man one day and call him a fraud the next'.[14] So Freuchen admitted to feeling 'very flattered' that Gibbs took him seriously, and gave him all the expert insight *Politiken* had not wanted to publish.

Gibbs wrote an article for the next day's *Chronicle* about how Freuchen 'utterly discredits Dr Cook's whole story, and says that he may be disproved on his own words by any man of science who knows the Arctic regions'. He set out Freuchen's view that it was implausible for the one sledge Cook said he had used to have carried enough food for his dogs (though, to be fair, Cook had said he had killed some of the dogs and fed them to the others), and that Cook could not have killed animals at 87 degrees latitude, as he claimed, because there were no animals above 84 degrees. Cook had also said he had not had a theodolite (an instrument for measuring angles); Freuchen did not believe he could have made accurate observations in the Arctic without one, and so would never be able to prove his claim.

While Gibbs continued his campaign against him, Cook was finally getting some quiet time in the Hotel Phoenix, attending to his correspondence and preparing for a speech he was to give after accepting the Royal Danish Geographical Society's gold medal that evening. The gold medal was a prestigious honour that had only been awarded to nine people before him, and the event was eagerly anticipated. Tickets to be one of the 1,200 people in the audience were changing hands for huge sums of money and *The New York Times* reported that 'almost everyone of position in Copenhagen is using his influence to the utmost to be included among the elect'.[15]

King Frederick and Crown Prince Christian were among the guests that evening, and Crown Prince Christian, the president of the society, presented Cook with his gold medal.[16] Then Cook stood in front of a map of the Arctic that was twice his height, the audience applauding him so enthusiastically that he had to wait a full five minutes for it to be quiet enough for him to start his lecture. Then he began talking in an easy, informal tone – 'he lectures as he converses in the drawing room', the *Daily Telegraph & Courier* correspondent thought.[17]

'It is too early to give the general results of the expedition,' Cook told the audience, as he began a speech that was as filled with graciousness as it was lacking in detail. 'Time is required to digest the work of polar effort,' he said. 'You have not allowed time in Copenhagen. This northward dash has occupied the minds of men for more than 300 years. Slowly and surely the ladder of latitudes has been climbed with various degrees of success. Experience was gained and each expedition profited by the misfortunes of its predecessors. The failure of one expedition led to the success of subsequent efforts … We are highly indebted to Nansen, Peary, and many Danish explorers for the last stages of Polar exploration. In my own case I am especially indebted to Captain Otto Sverdrup, who is here tonight.'

Cook went on to essentially repeat the account he had given in the *New York Herald*, adding that on the way back they had spent weeks on three-quarter rations – they only avoided starvation by managing to kill a bear – and were only able to make it back because they had a canvas boat with them. He finished by telling them they could read more detail about his achievement in his forthcoming book. The audience clapped in all the right places. When he got to the point in his story where he reached the Pole, they cheered so loudly he had to stop and wait for quiet, and there was more loud applause when he finished. Afterwards, Crown Prince Christian thanked him warmly and then the Royal Danish Geographical Society held a supper for him, its secretary toasting the 'discoverer of the North Pole'. Cook responded by thanking Denmark for a welcome that had made the last few days the happiest of his life.[18]

But for all the praise and as loud as the applause was, some people were disappointed he had not given more detail. Cook would later explain that 'because of the probability of the audience not understanding English, I confined myself to a brief narrative', but Gibbs, sitting in the audience, thought the lack of detail so suspicious that he was now left with no doubt at all. So after days of implying he thought Cook was lying, in his article about the lecture he came right out and said it:

Dr Frederick A Cook's lecture tonight before the King of Denmark and a great audience at the Geographical Society proves conclusively that his claim to have reached the North Pole belongs to the realm of fairy tales. It was all so very quick. In his own phrase, he 'climbed the ladder of latitude with lightning rapidity' although on the downward journey he beat about ice floes in a bewildered way, and put up for months in winter quarters, in spite of the daily risk of starvation, for his provisions would have been exhausted months before but for the convenient miracles of magic bears and birds. They appeared on the ice, and he was able to kill them with slings. In the same way a magic boat appeared. We had never heard of that boat before ... His way back was like a delirious dream of an Arctic explorer, zig-zagging and returning constantly upon his own path ... The great audience, which was anxious to hear about the North Pole, remained at that spot exactly two minutes on this personally conducted tour, and knew little more than what the map and geography primers had taught them as children. But they were solaced with Dr Cook's last words that if they desired further knowledge they would be able to buy his book, which would be published shortly.

There were many awkward pauses, and Dr Cook stumbled badly over his figures. His face was flushed, his forehead beaded with per-spiration. He had the grim look of a man determined to be believed as he drove that 'big nail' home with unconvincing, flashy phrases. I am in a position to state that the Danish Geographical Society, in limit-ing the lecture to an hour, asked Dr Cook to dilate especially on his travels near the pole and what Eskimos said and did on that April day. He did not do so tonight.[19]

By this stage, Gibbs's reporting of the story had become an exercise in prosecuting an argument rather than impartially weighing evidence, so he may not have been the best judge of Cook's lecture. Certainly, articles by some other journalists gave the impression they were listening to a different lecture. Where Gibbs described Cook's flushed face as he stumbled over his figures, the *New York Times* correspondent thought he 'told his story coolly and without hesitation'. But however well it was delivered, its lack of detail clearly caused disquiet. The *New York Times* correspondent wrote that Cook had 'added little to the information he had already given out',[20] while the *New York Sun* thought that 'never since he landed in Copenhagen, has the American explorer made so poor, so weak a showing'.[21] *The Times* was more charitable. While its correspondent agreed that 'he added nothing vital to his original published description of his journey', he thought 'his manner was exactly as calm and deliberate as it had been throughout'.[22]

Just as the lack of detail in Cook's lecture was raising questions and Gibbs's articles were becoming more explicit in their accusations of fraud, the attack on Cook's reputation was suddenly joined by his old friend Robert Peary. Polar explorers had a long history of observing a strict etiquette in their behaviour towards their fellow explorers, and Cook had observed this etiquette in his generous response to Peary's polar claim; he had followed his words of congratulation on hearing the news with a message to the *New York Herald* conveying 'my hearty congratulations upon his success'. But while Cook had told the journalists that 'there is glory enough for all of us', Peary was not the sort of man to want to share glory with anyone. Just as the dignitaries of the Royal Danish Geographical Society gathered to celebrate Cook's achievement, Peary tore up the rules of gentlemanly conduct by sending another telegram accusing the man whose life he had saved in Greenland of lying.

'Cook's story should not be taken too seriously,' Peary wrote. 'The two Eskimos who accompanied him say he went no distance north and not out of sight of land. Other members of the tribe corroborate their story.'

As word of Peary's intervention spread through the audience at the Royal Danish Geographical Society, the reaction was one of anxiety that the explorer they were honouring might really be a fraud, mixed with anger at Peary's undignified behaviour.

'Many advised me to reply in biting terms,' Cook later wrote. 'This I did not do; did not feel like doing.'[23] Instead of lowering himself to Peary's level, after his speech he reacted to news of the telegram with his usual civility. 'Commander Peary, of course, can say whatever he wishes,' Cook calmly told journalists. 'I am not accustomed to indulge in controversies. All I have to say about Commander Peary is that if he says he reached the North Pole, I believe he reached the North Pole.'[24]

Otto Sverdrup was less diplomatic when a journalist asked him about Peary's message. Sverdrup had experienced Peary's obnoxious personality firsthand: Peary had rudely refused Sverdrup's invitation of a cup of coffee when they had met in the Arctic, and had apparently attempted to name a cape in Greenland that Sverdrup had already discovered and named. 'It is like Peary,' Sverdrup said. 'Such an expression is very suitable for Peary's Arctic Club, but it deserves no notice by serious men. We all know Peary's boorishness.'[25]

9

THE MOST AMAZING MAN

An unease seemed to hang over Copenhagen as the next day dawned, the city's faith in Cook suddenly not quite so steadfast as it was. Peary added to the growing doubts with yet another message, sent to his wife but which quickly found its way to journalists: 'Good morning. Delayed by gale. Don't let Cook story worry you. Have him nailed.'[1]

The *Daily Mail* reported that the Danish public had become 'very uneasy' about Cook, and that 'a sudden and curious change of opinion has taken place in Danish scientific circles with regard to Dr Cook's claim as to the discovery of the pole, which is now as generally discredited as two days ago it was readily accepted'. And while *The New York Times* had initially been quite positive about Cook's lecture, it now reported that it had 'caused a profound disappointment because the people expected more convincing evidence than Dr Cook has given'.[2] The *Daily Chronicle*'s New York correspondent wrote that Peary's attack had 'practically shattered the claim of Dr Cook' in his home city, sending 'many of the waverers who were inclined to give Dr Cook the benefit of the doubt clean over to the opposition,'[3] while the *New York Post* told its readers that 'if Commander Peary proves his charges, Dr Cook will stand convicted of being the king of "fakers"'.[4]

Yet while the seed of doubt Gibbs had planted three days earlier had clearly grown, Cook was helped by the arrival in Copenhagen of his old friend Roald Amundsen, by now well known for having led the first expedition to make a ship voyage through the Northwest Passage between the Atlantic and the Pacific Oceans. Amundsen told the journalists waiting to speak to him that Cook was the most honest man he had ever met, and so if Cook said he had reached the Pole, he believed him. Amundsen dismissed the questions about why Cook did not have his observations in Copenhagen, saying it would have been safer for him to send his equipment to America because taking it to Europe would have risked it being damaged on the journey across Greenland.[5]

That day, Tuesday, 8 September, the *Daily Mail* correspondent asked Cook for his response to Peary's latest attack. 'I have been to the North Pole,' Cook told him. 'I do not want to enter into any controversy with Peary over the subject.'[6] His instinct was to ignore Peary, but that day Maurice Egan persuaded him to issue a statement in response to those who were accusing him of lying. 'One must not be astonished that I refused to furnish proof to various personages,' he wrote. 'I want to present the results of my work as a whole and not to private individuals, but to constituted bodies. I think those who have doubted my word will not doubt that of the geographical societies which I shall take for judges. I shall say no more. I hate this quarrel into which it is being sought to drag me. I am satisfied that I have done what I have done and know that in a little while no doubt will be possible.'[7]

In his article for the next day's *Daily Chronicle*, Gibbs also reported on how general opinion seemed to be moving away from Cook. He wrote, presumably with no small sense of satisfaction, that the lack of detail in Cook's lecture and Peary's allegations had 'staggered the people of Copenhagen' and that 'people who would have staked their lives upon his honesty were now full of the most terrible doubts'. 'The lecture was a fiasco of the first magnitude,' he went on, 'and seemed too obviously a story of the imagination, wildly improbable and unsupported by a shred of scientific facts, that those many explorers who were present and who stood by Cook now felt shattered in their belief. Some of them went to Cook early this morning and told him that unless he produced the strongest evidence of his claim within 24 hours they would denounce him as an imposter.'

Gibbs reported that Cook had agreed to do so.[8] 'That is a bold answer,' he wrote. 'When that was published this afternoon there were some people who doubted; again, they doubted their own doubts. One man said: "Either Cook must be proved an honest man before the world, or he must disappear."'

Gibbs did not say who these explorers were, or how he had heard about their ultimatum and Cook's reply to it. But we know that Carl Martin Norman Hansen, the explorer and poet who had been with Cook on the *Hans Egede*, was worried by the lecture's lack of detail and visited him the next morning to ask him to produce evidence he had reached the Pole, and Cook had apparently agreed to do so. So whether he told Gibbs himself or Gibbs heard it from someone else, Norman Hansen is likely to have been one of the explorers he was referring to.

That day, Gibbs joined two other journalists in visiting Alfred de Quervain, a 30-year-old meteorologist who was director of the Central Swiss Meteorological Institute. They wanted to interview him because he had just returned from his own expedition to Greenland and been one of Cook's fellow passengers on the *Hans Egede*. In de Quervain, they found a distinguished-looking man with a handlebar moustache, but he looked at them evasively from behind his pince-nez, and Gibbs wrote that in the interview that followed, 'every answer was drawn painfully and reluctantly from a man desiring to shield his friend but compelled by conscience to tell the truth'.

'Do you know Dr Cook well?' Gibbs asked him.

'I was four weeks with him upon his return,' said de Quervain. 'Coming back with him in the *Hans Egede*, we had long conversations.'

'Did he show you any of his observations?'

'No, but he said he would show them to me. I pointed out the importance of putting forward proofs to satisfy public opinion, and it was for that reason I suggested he should show me the observations, as, of course, I have had a long training and experience in these matters.'

'And did he?'

'No. I regret to say that when I asked him again, he said he would prefer not to do so.'

'He refused to do so?'

'Yes, he refused.'

'Are you sure he had any observations on board?'

'I could not be sure,' said de Quervain. 'He had a box on board, in which he said he had papers. Most of his books went by boat, Mr Whitney's boat, from Greenland to America.'

'Would it be possible for him to make imaginary observations?'

'I do not say it would be impossible, but it would be very difficult.'

'Did he have proper instruments with him?'

'He had a sextant and chronometers.'

'Was this sextant an ordinary one?'

'He told me that it was a better sextant than the ordinary one used in the Navy.'

'Do you know whether he had a theodolite with him?'

De Quervain seemed surprised at the question. 'No, he did not have one?' he asked.

'But, of course, this instrument was necessary for accurate observations?' Gibbs asked.

'Yes, for definite observations, but he could have made observations sufficient as rough proofs.'

'Has he brought his instruments to Copenhagen?'

'No, he sent them to America.'

'But is it not necessary to see and test these instruments before the value of the observations can be proved?'

'Strictly speaking, that is so.'

Gibbs thought it suspicious that Cook had refused to show de Quervain his observations. And if de Quervain was right that most of Cook's papers and his instruments were on their way to America, it raised the question of how Cook planned to produce proof of his achievement within the next 24 hours.

Wary after his experience with Strömgren, Gibbs got de Quervain to sign a statement confirming what he had said: 'I recognise that Cook, with whom I passed several weeks on board the *Hans Egede*, has given me the impression of a man who understands quite well how to take observations. Moreover, Knud Rasmussen, who passed some time with Cook after the return of the latter from the Pole, has received favourable evidence of Cook's story from Eskimos who knew two men who accompanied Cook and believe Cook has been to the Pole.'

De Quervain's statement was meant to show his support for Cook, but Gibbs thought de Quervain's claim that Cook had spoken to Knud Rasmussen since he had reached the Pole was 'startling', as this was the first time anyone had suggested the two explorers had met after Cook reached the Pole. He wrote in his article about the interview that 'Dr Cook has never referred to his meeting with Mr Rasmussen upon his homeward journey', and that 'Mr Rasmussen's letter to his wife suggests a direct contradiction of Dr Cook upon a material point, and from the lips of Mrs Rasmussen and of Mr Freuchen, the explorer in whose hands I first saw the letter, I heard the words that "Mr Rasmussen does not believe in Dr Cook's claim"'.

After interviewing de Quervain, Gibbs and another journalist went to the American Legation to try to talk to Cook himself. Cook was there and, perhaps surprisingly given what Gibbs had written about him, he agreed to talk to them. Cook greeted Gibbs civilly, though Gibbs thought it significant that when he handed around Maurice Egan's daughter's tea cakes, Cook refused to take one from him. Gibbs would later remember Egan as 'immensely courteous and kind',[9] but it was not a feeling that was reciprocated by the American minister. 'Philip Gibbs ... was looked on in sorrow and almost in anger by me, because, from the beginning, he declared that Dr Cook was not to be believed,' he wrote in his autobiography. 'To have an American citizen shown up in Denmark as a liar did not appeal to me as a representative of the United States.'[10]

Nothing that Cook said to Gibbs made him doubt his belief that Cook was a fraud, but he did leave their conversation greatly impressed by his coolness under pressure. One of the reasons Gibbs had originally suspected him of lying was because he had seemed to panic before going up onto the deck of the *Hans Egede*, but now Cook seemed preternaturally calm despite being at the centre of a huge global controversy. 'I must now say that this man Frederick Cook is the most remarkable, most amazing man I have ever met,' Gibbs wrote in his article for the next day's *Chronicle*. 'He calls me his enemy, but I have no personal animosity against him, and I will say honestly and warmly that I am filled with a sense of profound admiration for him. If he is an imposter he is also a very brave man – a man with such iron nerve, such miraculous self-control, and such magnificent courage in playing the game, that he will count for ever among the greatest imposters of the world. That and not the discovery of the North Pole shall be his claim to immortality. Here was this man doubted by all who had acclaimed him a hero, with his story strongly discounted by Peary, pursued by circumstantial evidence, and threatened within 24 hours by the almost certain possibility of final exposure, and yet he faced the world, defied criticism, and smiled and smiled again.'

Gibbs started his second interview with Cook by asking him to respond to Peary's allegation that he had not reached the Pole.

'I shall say very little about what Peary says,' Cook said. 'It does not matter to me. Wait a little while and you will see. I will produce my observations and records and instruments before the university tomorrow [at the ceremony where he would be awarded an honorary degree]. They shall see everything, and I shall prove the truth of my story to the world.'[11]

'Have you any original observations in Copenhagen?' Gibbs asked.

Cook seemed reluctant to answer. When Gibbs pressed him, he said: 'I have in Copenhagen results of my observations only, but my instruments and the working out of my observations have been packed with great care and are on their way to America.'

'Why have you not shown your observations and instruments to any Danish or other scientist?' Gibbs asked.

'I have not done so because I promised to show them later to the Danish–American geographical societies.'

'Why have you refused to show them to your friend Dr de Quervain?'

'He has seen the observations actually published.'

'Why did you ignore the request of the Danish Geographical Society to confine your lecture to an account of your journey in the neighbourhood of the Pole and to the behaviours and conversation of the Eskimos when near and at the Pole?'

'There were no reasons to do so now,' Cook said. 'That could come later in my book.'

As well as talking to Cook, Gibbs spent two hours with him in the drawing room of the American Legation, studying his quarry as he was called on by visitor after visitor who Gibbs thought seemed doubtful about his claim. 'Ceremoniously polite he stood among them, shaking hands, bowing and smiling,' Gibbs wrote. 'He was haggard, and there were deep lines upon his face, but his hand was perfectly steady as he took a cup of tea and still he smiled.'

Gibbs ended his article about the interview by repeating one of Cook's statements to emphasise its significance: 'I have in Copenhagen the results of my observations only.' This, Gibbs thought, meant it would be impossible for him to produce his proofs before the university the following day, despite having just told Gibbs he would do so. 'I say Cook cannot prove his story tomorrow or the day after,' Gibbs wrote. 'I say to Cook and the world that there are no proofs whatever that he reached the Pole. It is impossible for Frederick Cook to present proofs tomorrow.'

That day, Gibbs also found himself in the unusual position of being the subject of newspaper interest himself. The *Politiken* newspaper was one of Cook's fullest-throated supporters, but now that questions about his claim were becoming louder, it wanted to interview the journalist who had been suspicious from the beginning. Gibbs agreed, believing it telling that 'Danish journalists came to interview the English journalist who had been alone in his disbelief' after they had previously 'upheld Dr Cook and had denounced the *Daily Chronicle*, and me personally, for the daily criticism of Dr Cook's story'. In his article for the next day's *Chronicle*, Gibbs wrote that the *Politiken* interview had been the 'only amusing thing in a day which has been too exciting and strenuous', and he used it to set out his case directly to the Danish public, many of whom had only read the coverage in the pro-Cook Danish press.

'I do not think Dr Cook has been to the North Pole,' he told the journalist. 'When I left London, I believed he had made the journey, but since I have met the American doctor my opinion has changed. The first thing I asked him for was permission to see his observation books. He replied that he could not show them to me, as he had already sent most of them to America. This greatly surprised me. Why should he part with these precious books? Since then, I have visited many places to see if anyone has seen Dr Cook's observation books. But no, no one has seen them. I told Commander Hovgaard I was astonished the Geographical Society could accept a man who brought no more proof with him than his own words. I think they should have waited until the books were on the table ... There are also now the telegrams from Peary, which seem to be doing away with Dr Cook's claim that the Eskimos will testify in his favour. Dr Cook has also stated that Knud Rasmussen would be able to support him, but Knud Rasmussen's letters do not give him this support. No, until Dr Cook presents better evidence, the impartial observer must come to the conclusion that the doctor has not been to the North Pole.'[12]

After finishing the interview, Gibbs wrote his article about his conversations with Cook and de Quervain and went to the telegraph office to send it back to London. As he walked back to his hotel through Copenhagen's busy, tram-filled streets, Gibbs reflected on how after the reports about Strömgren and Torp had threatened his career, public opinion now finally seemed to be moving in his favour. But as he walked across a square, he was approached by a Danish journalist clutching a newspaper. The journalist asked him if he had seen the news. Gibbs looked at the newspaper and saw it was about Dagmar Rasmussen, and the journalist explained that the article said she had given a statement to a Danish news agency disputing the accuracy of Gibbs's report about her husband's letter.

As the journalist translated the article for him, Gibbs learned with mounting horror that Dagmar Rasmussen had claimed Gibbs was wrong to say her husband had denied meeting the Inuit who had accompanied Cook, and that she insisted Knud Rasmussen did believe in Cook's claim.[13] 'In my interviews with the *Daily Chronicle*'s two correspondents, again and again I stressed that the only opinion my husband had written expressed the strongest conviction that Dr Cook had been to the North Pole,' Dagmar Rasmussen wrote in her statement.[14]

Gibbs could hardly believe what he was reading. He had enjoyed spending time with Dagmar Rasmussen and Peter Freuchen, and they had helped him with his reporting of the story more than anyone else in Copenhagen. He could not understand why she was now accusing him of lying. After days spent questioning Cook's truthfulness, it was Gibbs's own honesty that was now in question and he found himself once again on the defensive as news of Dagmar Rasmussen's statement swept the city. One newspaper correspondent in Copenhagen later reported that 'the people have perhaps been more stirred by the vague tales about Rasmussen's letters to his wife than anything else'.[15]

Feeling panic rising within him, Gibbs went to look for Dagmar Rasmussen and Freuchen but could not find them. In fact, he would never see Dagmar Rasmussen again.

Then Gibbs remembered the piece of paper Freuchen had used to copy the extract of the letter, and on which the *Daily Chronicle*'s Copenhagen correspondent Oscar Hansen had translated it into English. He had not thought anything more of this piece of paper once he had finished writing his article about it, assuming it would have no further use. But he now realised it could be his only proof that he was telling the truth. He could not find it in his pockets, and so went back to his hotel room and searched through the pieces of paper scattered over the floor. Finally, on his hands and knees, he shouted in triumph as he found it screwed up under his bed.

Gibbs went to see Oscar Hansen, who signed a statement confirming he had translated the text Freuchen had copied from the letter, and then he found a news agency editor who was prepared to confirm that the other handwriting on the piece of paper was Freuchen's. He then wrote his response and delivered it to the news agency that had published Dagmar Rasmussen's statement.

In it, he set out his defence:

I regret that Mrs Rasmussen has denied the truth of the information which I say she gave to me and which I published in my paper, the *Daily Chronicle*. Mrs Rasmussen and her husband's friend and brother explorer, Mr Peter Freuchen, told me, not once only but several times, that Mr Rasmussen did not believe Cook's claim, and that they also doubted the truth of Cook's story. The conversations I had with them were not alone, but in the presence of Mr Oscar Hansen, who confirms this statement. Mr Hansen read my messages to the *Daily Chronicle* before they were telegraphed, and now agrees that they gave an accurate account of the information given to me by Mrs Rasmussen and Mr Freuchen. The words which I quoted from Mr Rasmussen's letter to his wife were written down for my use in Danish by Mr Freuchen, translated into English by Mr Hansen and confirmed by Mrs Rasmussen, to whom I showed them. I still have the document in my possession in Mr Freuchen's handwriting, which I am prepared to produce before a committee.

The words in Mr Freuchen's handwriting were exactly as follows: 'My first feeling when I heard about Dr Cook was an enormous disappointment and I am sorry.' It goes on to say that Knud Rasmussen has not spoken with the two Eskimos who were there at the North Pole, and Dr Cook had sent the other 10 back. If there is any doubt that these words were sent by Mr Rasmussen, I very earnestly beg Mrs Rasmussen, whose friendship I have very much esteemed, to produce her husband's letter before a committee of Danish gentlemen. If, then, it is shown that no such words are contained in the letter I can only say that I was wrongly informed by Mrs Rasmussen, and by Mr Freuchen, in whose handwriting the words are now in my possession. In that case I will withdraw fully on that point; but it seems to me remarkable that if the letter contains a defence of Cook it should not have been published in the Danish papers when such defence would have been immensely valuable.

As well as giving his statement to the news agency, Gibbs sent it to the *Daily Chronicle*. 'I only wish to add to my English readers that there has been much conversation in Copenhagen about this letter,' he wrote. '"When Mrs Rasmussen hears from her husband," it was said, "we shall know a good deal." But there has been a strange silence about that letter – a long letter which I have seen and handled in the presence of Mrs Rasmussen and Mr Freuchen and Mr Hansen. That silence has only been broken by the damning words published by me and obtained by me in the way I have described.'

Following Gibbs's response, Dagmar Rasmussen would issue another statement, making clear her anger with Gibbs but also attempting to draw a line under the controversy: 'After Mr Gibbs's last statement, I give up taking him seriously and refuse to answer not only to this, but to anything his imagination might further attribute to me.'

But Peter Freuchen offered a partial explanation for what had happened when he issued a statement admitting that, having already blundered over the date of the Spring Equinox, he had made an error that was at least partly to blame for the controversy. 'I must declare that this little misunderstanding originates with me,' he wrote. 'With Mrs Knud Rasmussen's permission, I wrote the first of the two quotes and then on the same piece of paper wrote that Knud Rasmussen had not spoken to the two Eskimos, etc. The contents of the sentence is true, but due to my inability to express myself in English, Mr Gibbs also thought this sentence had been written by Knud Rasmussen. Hence the whole misunderstanding, which I deeply regret.'

Presumably, Freuchen had somehow heard that Rasmussen had not spoken to the Inuit, and so thought it would be helpful to write this on the piece of paper after copying the extract from Rasmussen's letter, but Gibbs had wrongly assumed it was part of the letter. But Freuchen's error does not fully explain the misunderstanding. The day before Dagmar Rasmussen showed Gibbs the letter, a correspondent from *Le Matin* reported that she had received a letter from Knud Rasmussen, in which he had written that 'I was never so much moved in my life as by the success of Cook, for I hoped to carry off this triumph myself'.

The *Le Matin* article quoted Dagmar Rasmussen as saying her husband had thought only Inuit would be able to reach the Pole, and that he put Cook's success down to him having lived like an Inuit. 'My husband was the first to congratulate Dr Cook, and he listened to the testimony of the Eskimos, which was by no means negligible,' she told the journalist from *Le Matin*. 'They do not understand the use of instruments, but they know how to make observations of solar light. My husband does not doubt in any way Dr Cook's veracity. He is even mortified not to have performed the feat himself. He nonetheless congratulates the great explorer.'[16]

Gibbs would later come to believe that Dagmar Rasmussen had been got at. 'I learned afterwards that she had weakened under great political and social pressure from high quarters,' Gibbs wrote. 'I have long since forgiven her.' But while it may have suited him to believe she had been pressured into falsely denying his accurate story, this belief is undermined by the fact that Knud Rasmussen really does seem to have believed Cook had reached the Pole. The following month, he forwarded *The New York Times* a message he had sent to Cook when he heard about his achievement: 'My heartiest congratulations on your happy North Pole journey. Your victory is the greatest in the history of Arctic exploration.' They are not the words of a man who thought Cook was lying.

When he wrote to *The New York Times*, Rasmussen also explained why he had not commented publicly before: 'As I got the impression that he was going to take toward eventual doubters a tone of superiority, which he had a perfect right to do, I thought a defence from me would be out of place, and I preferred to keep quiet. But now, after the information which I have from the newspapers which go to September 9 [the day after Dagmar Rasmussen's statement denying the truth of Gibbs's article] I think the moment has come to speak ... It is, of course, impossible for me to give absolute proofs that Cook, a single white man with two young Eskimos, has been to the Pole. It must necessarily be more or less a matter of belief ... [but] there will always, in such big, complicated things as a North Pole journey, be a number of small points which, without constituting absolute proof, still on the whole will give a picture of fact that leaves out all doubt.'

Rasmussen went on to set out a case for why he believed Cook had reached the Pole that was far more convincing than anything Cook himself had so far managed. He wrote that friends of the two Inuit who had accompanied Cook had said they had headed north and that they had benefited from good ice and good weather. The two Inuit had apparently confirmed they had reached a point where the sun did not disappear at all, and that it was autumn by the time they decided to go into winter quarters, which tallied with Cook's claim that they reached their winter quarters in September 1908. The Inuit were also said to have corroborated Cook's account of fighting muskoxen and walrus without ammunition, and to have told friends they had gone far from the shore and were surprised when Cook told them they had reached the Pole, because the ice there seemed no different to the ice they had already travelled over. This led Rasmussen to think Cook must have decided to turn back because he believed they had reached their goal, rather than because the conditions made it too difficult to continue.

'The above facts must be looked upon as strong confirmation for Cook,' Rasmussen concluded. 'Personally, I want to express my unreserved admiration for Dr Cook. A man who with his bare hands has passed a winter at Cape Sparbo [at Devon Island in northern Canada], a man who on his feet has taken a walk to Annoatok [in northern Greenland] through deep snow, through twisting ice and utter darkness, that man certainly deserves to have been the first at the Pole. His name is Frederick Cook. No one in the world can name him a swindler.'[17]

So if Rasmussen was so sure Cook had reached the Pole, why was Gibbs convinced he did not believe it? Why did Gibbs claim Dagmar Rasmussen had told him that neither she nor her husband believed in Cook, when the previous day she had apparently told *Le Matin* that Knud Rasmussen did believe Cook's claim? And why did she give *Le Matin* the impression Knud Rasmussen had spoken to the two Inuit and then the next day Freuchen write that he had not? As with many details of Cook's trip north and the weeks that followed his arrival in Copenhagen, we will never know for sure. But the most plausible explanation is that Knud Rasmussen really did believe Cook, but that Dagmar Rasmussen did not. Freuchen certainly thought Cook was lying, and perhaps Dagmar Rasmussen was either convinced by him or nodded along with his critique of Cook in a way that gave Gibbs the impression she agreed with him. The fact that the text in question was being hurriedly translated between Danish, French and English must have also increased the potential for confusion. And by the time he was shown the extract of the letter, Gibbs was so determined to prove Cook was lying that he did not stop to ask himself if the extract from Knud Rasmussen's letter might have another meaning.

This was *Politiken*'s conclusion. When it reported on the controversy, it pointed to an article Freuchen had written about the same letter as evidence that Gibbs had misinterpreted Knud Rasmussen's meaning. 'Mr Gibbs … draws particular attention to the point in Mr Freuchen's manuscript that said it was "an enormous disappointment and I am sorry", which Mr Gibbs sent his paper in literal translation,' *Politiken* explained. 'This is very true, and the same words are also found quoted in the article Mr Freuchen wrote on Tuesday in *Politiken* about Knud Rasmussen's letters. But Mr Gibbs forgets what followed it. From Freuchen's own story it seems clear what Knud Rasmussen meant. We quote: "My first impression was an enormous disappointment and I am sorry. Who can immediately take a detached approach to a matter that touches the loneliest string? It was a road that was blocked. The North Pole has been reached, so there is no need for more effort there."'

Given its support for Cook, *Politiken* was clearly looking for evidence that he was telling the truth, just as Gibbs was desperate to prove he was lying. But it does seem that Gibbs read Knud Rasmussen's wistfulness at the realisation that Cook's achievement had ended his own chance of being first to the North Pole and misinterpreted it as casting doubt on Cook's truthfulness.

10

I SHOW YOU MY HANDS

Anyone reading the *Daily Chronicle* over the previous three days would have been all too aware that its editors were deeply suspicious about Cook's claim to have reached the North Pole. But while Gibbs had openly called Cook a liar, the newspaper itself had not yet done so. But as well as the accumulating circumstantial evidence against him, the *Chronicle*'s editors thought that with each day that passed without Cook producing proof, the less plausible it seemed that he might be telling the truth. And when Gibbs's article about his interviews with de Quervain and Cook arrived at the *Chronicle*'s London office, they decided the time for cautious doubting was over. The time had come to directly accuse Cook of fraud.

So on Thursday, 9 September, the *Chronicle*, not yet aware that Dagmar Rasmussen was denying the truth of Gibbs's article about her husband's letter, published a long and damning indictment of Cook:

> Our readers have observed that from the first moment when Dr Cook put forward his claim we have adopted an attitude of steady scepticism. Perhaps there is something in the atmosphere of the office of the *Daily Chronicle* that is inimical to charlatans. It was an atmosphere which just 11 years ago was fatal to the pretensions of Louis de Rougemont [a hoaxer whose false account of exploring Australasia the *Chronicle* had exposed in 1898] ... A duty was performed then

which it seems we must discharge once more. It is a duty which is undertaken with a profound sense of responsibility. As long as there was the slightest chance that we might be guilty of an injustice to a man – mistaken, perhaps, but innocent – we have held our hands. The time has arrived when any further display of magnanimity would be useless, and might be misconstrued.

We now charge Dr Cook with having fabricated all the statements of any significance with which he has supported his claim to have reached the North Pole. We charge him with attempting an imposture upon the world, and with the knowledge that he could not long sustain the pretence. In doing this – and it is not the least item to his discredit – he has betrayed the trust of a generous people and outraged their hospitality. The profound sympathy of all right-thinking people will be expressed towards the King of Denmark and his subjects that unkind circumstances should have brought this man to their friendly shores.

Looking back upon this extraordinary career, not yet a week old, and now ended, the main cause of wonder is that it lasted so long. Here was a man, with no credentials except his unsupported word, whose reputation as an explorer, moreover, was not calculated to inspire confidence, who yet was able for the space of several days to delude a large proportion of mankind in all parts of the world that he was all he pretended to be. Yet at the outset he came in contact with scientists and explorers and geographers who might reasonably have been expected to put their finger upon any weak points in his case.

A strange psychological problem is suggested by the fact that Dr Cook's claims were accepted – even by men accustomed to analyse and dissect evidence – entirely on trust. He submitted no proof except his simple statement that he had discovered the Pole, supported – if it can be called supported – only by such data as were within reach of anybody with the most elementary knowledge of Polar conditions. That Dr Cook is equipped with a most plausible manner is evident from the fact that he convinced a body of hardened journalists, collected from almost every capital of Europe, of his bona-fides. We believe we are right in saying that of the assembled regiments, only one – the Special Correspondent of *The Daily Chronicle*, who had previously had the privilege of cross-examining Dr Cook on board the *Hans Egede* – was sceptical as to the virtue of his pretensions. Most of the journalists became at once not only partisans, but enthusiastic partisans, of the Polar hero ...

Our readers will have recognised that from the beginning – as early as Friday last week – we adopted an attitude which was severely judicial ... He has remained silent. We have given him every opportunity of replying to these criticisms ... He has been given every chance both in Copenhagen and elsewhere of making good his claim to be regarded as the man who first reached the Pole. He has lamentably failed to appreciate the seriousness of the position in which he finds himself. Such a position cannot be indefinitely prolonged, and Dr Cook must be made to realise that his imposture is now at an end.[1]

For a newspaper as influential as the *Daily Chronicle* to condemn Cook so excoriatingly was a major new development in the story. In unequivocally accusing him of lying, it was signalling not only that it did not believe him, but that it thought the evidence against him was now so strong that it was prepared to run the risk of a potentially expensive libel suit.

At the same time as the *Chronicle* was publishing its editorial in Britain, in Copenhagen *Politiken* published its interview with Gibbs. Headlined 'Where I do not believe in Dr Cook', its article presented Gibbs as one of the *Chronicle*'s 'most skilful reporters', whose articles about Cook had 'aroused so much controversy'. While its article set out his case, it made it clear it thought he was still in the minority in doubting Cook's story. 'We owe it to Dr Cook to add that only a few of the other correspondents distrust him,' it reported. 'With Mr Stead at the helm, they declare themselves almost all Cookites.'[2]

If the text left any doubt as to what *Politiken* thought of Gibbs, the article was accompanied by a drawing of him that seemed designed to make him look as villainous as possible. It shows Gibbs sitting on a chair in a dark jacket and formal high collar, his face cloaked in shadow and his mouth turned down slightly as he looks out at the reader from the corners of his eyes. When Gibbs came to look back on his time in Copenhagen many years later, he would still remember this 'murderous-looking portrait of me'.[3]

The article confirmed Gibbs's position as what he described as 'the most unpopular man in Copenhagen', causing such outrage among Cook's supporters that he found himself threatened with physical violence. The explorer and poet Carl Martin Norman Hansen may have been worried by the lack of detail in Cook's lecture earlier in the week, but he had been sufficiently persuaded by Cook's reassurances to be furious about Gibbs's interview. Norman Hansen was particularly angry that it gave the impression Gibbs had interviewed Cook alone on the *Hans Egede* rather than as part of a group of journalists, and so he went to the *Politiken* office to set the record straight. He told one of its journalists that Gibbs had been little more than an 'attentive listener' on the *Hans Egede*, and gave them a signed statement to publish in the next day's newspaper: 'I charge Mr Philip Gibbs of the *Daily Chronicle* with having given an untruthful account of his first meeting with Dr Cook onboard S/S *Hans Egede* in the early morning of September 4.'

Politiken duly printed it, reporting that Norman Hansen's allegation was 'as unsettling as Mr Gibbs's reporting on Knud Rasmussen's testimony'. It also claimed Gibbs had failed to give a balanced report of his interview with Cook on the *Hans Egede* and had instead extracted 'fragments of an interview to draw exactly the picture he wants, when for the other journalists present the interview made exactly the opposite impression'. 'It is perhaps not a bad approach for a young journalist who wishes to make his name known,' *Politiken* continued, 'but in the long run it is unsuitable for a discussion which has assumed such a serious character as The Battle for the North Pole.'

Being accused of dishonesty was bad enough, but the journalist who showed Gibbs the *Politiken* article told him that by publicly accusing him of lying, Norman Hansen was challenging Gibbs to a fight to defend Cook's honour.

'What's it all about?' Gibbs asked, seeing his name but unable to read the Danish text.

'Norman Hansen challenges you to a duel,' the journalist said. 'He has constituted himself the champion of Dr Cook.'

It was a challenge Gibbs had no intention of accepting. 'I may have blanched,' he later remembered. 'He was a tall man, six foot three or so in his socks, and very powerful. I am five foot six or so in my boots. If we met, I should die.'[4]

Fearing Norman Hansen might attack him, and with Norman Hansen, Dagmar Rasmussen and now *Politiken* all questioning his integrity, Gibbs was by now in a constant state of anxiety. But he could at least take comfort from the fact that more newspapers were now doubting Cook's story. 'As each day passes Dr Cook's claim is the subject of increasing scepticism,' the *Manchester Guardian* reported. 'The case for the sceptics has gone far enough to be entitled to receive an answer which shows some conception of the gravity of the situation. Let Dr Cook produce his instruments; let him show his critics his diaries and the manuscripts of his book. To do so is his only means of regaining general credence.'[5]

That day, Cook also found himself under attack on an entirely new front. The *Chronicle* may have disparaged his previous achievements in exploration as 'not calculated to inspire confidence', but this was unfair to a man who had spent winters in the Arctic and Antarctica and was the first known person to both circumnavigate and reach the summit of Mount McKinley. In fact, it was this impressive record of achievement and the esteem in which he was held by explorers such as Roald Amundsen and Knud Rasmussen that were among the strongest reasons for believing he was telling the truth about the Pole. If he had achieved all those things, why could he not have reached the North Pole, too? And why would someone who had accomplished so much risk their reputation with so reckless a lie?

But across the Atlantic, journalists in New York had been looking into his past achievements and what they found raised doubts about whether his previous career was all he claimed it to be. They had found that shortly after his second McKinley expedition, Professor Herschel Parker, who had been on the expedition but turned back early, had publicly questioned whether he had really reached the summit. His comments had been reported at the time but were barely noticed, and he had apparently later been persuaded that Cook really had got to the top.[6] But with Cook now having claimed the biggest prize in exploration, Parker spoke to *The New York Times* and once again raised doubts about his McKinley claim. 'It is with great reluctance that I am compelled to say that Dr Frederick A Cook has not made a satisfactory explanation or submitted corroborative evidence that he made the ascent of Mount McKinley,' he said. 'I do not know whether Dr Cook climbed Mount McKinley or not. This I know, that he reports that the mountain was 20,390 feet high, but I am unable to say how he made his observations, inasmuch as I took back with me the hypsometers [instruments for measuring height] and he had only one or two aneroid barometers [for measuring air pressure], which would measure only about 18,000 feet. A man of science naturally asks why he did not make photographs of the other summit of Mount McKinley, only a short distance away, and of views about him ... These photographs of the approaches to Mount McKinley summit in themselves would have settled the question. Dr Cook must have readily appreciated that in an undertaking of this kind, that of making a world's record, some necessary proof would be fairly asked by scientific men. As I say, I am a friend of Dr Cook, but in matters of this kind scientific proof is needed. If Dr Cook has climbed Mount McKinley, then he has made a bad case of it, as the lawyers say.'[7]

As well as Parker's comments to *The New York Times*, Fred Printz, one of the guides on Cook's McKinley expeditions, had told the *New York Sun* that Cook had lied about reaching the top and had actually climbed a smaller peak and taken photographs there that he had then passed off as having been taken at McKinley's summit. 'I am just as sure as I'm living that Dr Cook never saw the North Pole,' he said. 'Any man who would make the representations he did as to his alleged ascent of Mount McKinley is capable of making the statements credited to him in the press about the North Pole achievement. I made two trips to Alaska with Cook in company with [fellow guide Ed] Barrill and Walter P Miller of the Seattle Post-Intelligencer, who acted as photographer ... He evidently sized us up, and taking Barrill ascended an adjoining mountain, a mere foothill in comparison ... Miller and I were detailed to make a side trip to secure game heads for the Smithsonian Institution. Barrill told me afterward that Cook offered to give him hush money. Dr Cook agreed to pay me $150 and expenses on the trip, but he did not even pay my expenses, and I had to borrow money to get home ... On reaching Seattle the papers were filled with Dr Cook's dope and a banquet was given in his honour. Miller and I said nothing in contradiction, hoping by keeping mum Cook would eventually pay us.'

Parker's doubts and Printz's accusation were significant for the North Pole story because, if Cook had lied about climbing McKinley, there was every reason to think he was lying about the North Pole, too. But the only person who had been with him when he claimed to have reached the top of McKinley was Ed Barrill, and Barrill was refusing to say anything. All he would tell journalists was that he would make a sworn statement once Cook was back in the United States.

Cook had planned to go from Copenhagen to Brussels and then back to America, but with the mounting controversy it was announced he would instead be leaving Copenhagen the next day to head for New York.

The *Daily Chronicle*'s damning editorial and the questions about his McKinley claim could hardly have come at a worse time for the University of Copenhagen, which just then was putting the finishing touches to preparations for its ceremony to award Cook his honorary degree later that day. We can only wonder what was going through the minds of university officials as they prepared a public demonstration of their faith in Cook just as newspapers in London and New York were accusing him of lying and with still no sign of the proof he had apparently promised. But whatever doubts they may have had, they decided to go ahead with the ceremony. With a crowd waiting outside, an audience of more than 1,000 people that included royalty and some of the most eminent explorers and scientists in the country gathered for a ceremony filled with all the pomp and grandeur the ancient university could muster.[8]

Gibbs was in the audience to watch Cook bestowed with one of Copenhagen's most prestigious honours. 'The scene in the University was unforgettable,' he wrote in his article about it. 'The hall was filled by Danish men of science and exploration – men with heads that Franz Hals might have painted – and on a dais were Princes and Princesses.' As he had done on the *Hans Egede* and at the banquet, Gibbs spent the ceremony with his eyes fixed on Cook, hoping for something in his expression or body language that might offer a clue as to the thoughts that lay behind his composed visage. 'I watched him as he sat there, while solemn music played for nearly half an hour in the dead silence of the assembly, and while Danish professors made long speeches, not a word of which he could understand,' Gibbs wrote. 'It was a strange face – powerful, with hard lines about the eyes and mouth, with the look of a man not receiving a high honour, but undergoing his worst ordeal. He sat gnawing his moustache and lips; and behind him sat rows of grave men, looking serious and anxious. One felt that the accusations and suspicions of the world were in the thoughts of all these men and of Cook himself.'

University Rector Carl Torp, who had recommended Cook for the degree, gave a speech praising his courage and self-sacrifice in going where no human had gone before. 'Whether your scientific research will rank very highly or not, the faculty gives you this degree in recognition of your great achievements in exploration and the qualities you have shown herein,' Torp said.[9] Torp then presented him with his degree as the audience applauded loudly.

Cook then climbed the dais to give his acceptance speech. He thanked the university and said he accepted the degree as testimony to the genuineness of his journey. He promised that once he was back in New York he would send the university his complete records so it could pass judgement on his claim, and said he planned to send a ship to Greenland to bring back Etukishook and Ahwelsh, the two Inuit who had accompanied him to the Pole, so they could corroborate his story. Then he paused, seeming to reflect for a moment on how he was accepting the degree at a time when his honesty was being so widely questioned. He held out his hands, showing his palms to the audience. 'I can say no more, I can do no more,' he said dramatically, his voice full of emotion. 'I show you my hands.'

In Gibbs's article about the ceremony, he admitted Cook had spoken 'squarely and bravely', and Gibbs thought Cook seemed so genuine as he showed his palms to the audience that a wave of doubt washed over him and he found himself worrying that perhaps he really was telling the truth.[10]

Whatever doubts the audience may have harboured, they again applauded Cook loudly, and then Cook walked out of the building to the cheers of the large crowd waiting outside. Whatever allegations were being levelled at him in newspapers around the world, to the public in Copenhagen, at least, Cook was still very much the hero of the North Pole.

After leaving the university, Cook returned to the Hotel Phoenix to change for dinner at Ledreborg Castle outside Copenhagen, where the Danish prime minister was to host him on his final evening in Denmark. At the hotel, a *Politiken* journalist asked him for his response to Gibbs's interview with *Politiken*.

'What he said to *Politiken* astonished me, but I do not think the questions he raised have embarrassed me,' he said.

While Cook prepared to dine with the prime minister, Gibbs was writing his article about the university ceremony. In it, he acknowledged that Cook's assurances had seemed heartfelt, but then continued his attack on him by arguing that the true test of his speech was whether it had fulfilled his promise of the previous day to produce proof that he had reached the Pole. It had failed to do so, Gibbs told his readers, and this single fact was as damning as any other piece of evidence against him:

He did not present any of his papers whatever for examination. He did not show any of the contents of the mysterious box seen by

Dr de Quervain on board the *Hans Egede*, or of the mysterious black bag seen by, but not opened in the presence of, Mr Sverdrup. He did not show anything at all. He only made assertions as he has always made them, and therefore I say that everything I have said since the beginning of this strange mystery, everything I produced which throws doubt upon his story, every criticism I have made in all sincerity, has been fully and absolutely justified. I have said Cook will not produce his proofs. He refuses to produce them. He does not possess a shred of proof, at any rate within reach of civilisation, and not at Copenhagen, to which he came expecting and receiving honours. For these assertions on my part, based on evidence and signed statements, and interviews in the presence of witnesses, I have been denounced in the Danish papers, and have been a marked man in Copenhagen. Yet I will leave my readers to say whether I have gone beyond truth and justice.

Dr Cook has falsified the hopes of his friends. Though, as I admit, the faith of most of them is again still strong in him, he has contradicted his own words again and again. He has not produced those papers which he said he would produce, and he has utterly failed to do any of those things which the world expects from a man who comes with a story incredible except by proof. Once again I say, until Frederick Cook produces his proofs he has no right to be believed.

Gibbs was clearly right that if Cook had promised to produce proof within 24 hours, he had failed to make good on it. But the previous day, Gibbs had also written that Cook's promise had been forced out of him by unnamed explorers who had threatened to denounce him, and Gibbs now failed to explain why those explorers had not come forward to accuse him of lying. Even today, it is a question to which there is no obvious answer.

Gibbs sent his article to London and then a few hours later telegraphed an update on Cook's promise to send a ship to Greenland to bring back the two Inuit: 'I have very good reason to believe that

Captain Sverdrup will not take out a ship to Cape York to fetch back the Eskimos, this idea already having been abandoned.'

In the *Daily Chronicle*'s editorial accompanying Gibbs's article, this promise to send the ship to Greenland was presented as just another lie to add to the long list of lies Cook had told since his first telegram from the Shetland Islands. 'The whole of these manoeuvres seem to be an expedient to gain time and to postpone the evil day when doubt will become absolute certainty,' it argued. 'But there is good ground for thinking that this point will be cleared up without further intervention from Dr Cook himself.'[11]

11

A WILD DREAM

The following afternoon, on Friday, 10 September, Frederick Cook left the Hotel Phoenix and was driven in a convoy of three cars to the harbour, where a boat was waiting to start him on his journey back to the United States.

In terms of world opinion, the previous day's university ceremony had done little to stop the waning of Cook's credibility and there was a growing sense that it was Robert Peary who had the better claim to be the Pole's discoverer. 'We have now a categorical and credible narrative from one explorer and no attempt at substantiation from the other,' argued that day's *Pall Mall Gazette*. 'In view of Dr Cook's unnecessary reticence we may fairly place his claim aside; judgement for the present goes against him by default.'[1] And as Cook was preparing to leave Denmark, Peary renewed his attack on him with yet another telegram, this time to *The New York Times*: 'Do not trouble about Cook's story or attempt to explain any discrepancies in his statements. The affair will settle itself. He has not been at the Pole on 21 April 1908, or at any other time. He has simply handed the public a gold brick. These statements are made advisedly and I have proof of them.'[2]

But whatever doubts existed in the world at large and despite the growing ominousness of Peary's interventions, thousands of people lined the streets on the way to the harbour that afternoon to cheer him and wave goodbye. When they reached the quay, Cook found an echo of the scenes that had greeted his arrival six days earlier, with the harbour filled with boats flying the American flag and a crowd of so many thousands of people that some of them struggled to avoid being pushed into the water.[3] The crowd broke through the police barriers and threw flowers at his car. 'The cheers that greeted him were as much a tribute to his personal character as to his epoch-making exploit,' Maurice Egan later wrote. 'Kindly, simple, firm, and sincere, he had, in a short time, made the sons of Vikings love him.'[4]

Cook boarded a boat called the *Melchior*, which was to take him to Kristiansand in Norway (he was to be accompanied for this first leg of the journey by Amundsen and Sverdrup), from where he would take a steamer to New York. When he had arrived the previous Saturday, he had not had much more with him than the clothes he was wearing; now, his entourage loaded five large trunks of luggage onto the boat.[5] There was a reception on board the *Melchior*, where dignitaries including Maurice Egan and Professor Carl Torp bid Cook farewell, and Admiral Andreas du Plessis de Richelieu gave a speech assuring him their faith in him remained undimmed by the torrent of negative newspaper articles. 'Green-eyed envy and jealousy are doing their envenomed work, but we in Denmark believe in you absolutely,' he said.

Cook gave a short speech in response. 'Since I cannot reach home on an American steamer or an expedition vessel, it is fitting that I should go home on a steamer of the land which has given me such happy days,' he told them. 'You have made my return so happy that the tortures of the past are forgotten. You have been my friends. You have fought my battles. With a full heart I say farewell to the people of Denmark.' He then gave Reuters news agency a farewell message to the Danish people: 'As I am about to leave Copenhagen, the first place in the civilised world upon which I set foot on my return from the Pole, I desire to express to the Danish people my very high appreciation of the kindness shown to me on all sides. I thank you one and all for your good feelings.'

As he was about to leave, a journalist asked him to respond to Peary's latest attack.

'I am perfectly willing to put my records before the American Coast and Geodetic Survey to be compared with those of Commander Peary, but I do not see why I should ask for such a comparison first,' he said, adding that all he wanted to do now was to get home to see his wife and children, and to finish his work.

Cook shouted a few words of goodbye to the crowd and then the *Melchior* departed. He went out onto the bridge so the cheering crowd could get a last look at him as it slowly disappeared into the distance.[6]

One member of the crowd who was not cheering was Philip Gibbs. He had stood under the gangway as Cook accepted the good wishes of the Danish people, and as he watched the *Melchior* leave, he realised his involvement in by far the biggest story of his career so far was coming to an end. Over the last few days, he had intensely observed Cook at every opportunity and interviewed him twice, and the sight of him standing on the bridge of the *Melchior* was the last that Gibbs would ever see of him. While Frederick Cook's story still had some distance to run, its next chapter would be told by New York's journalists.

After the *Melchior* had disappeared from view, Gibbs continued to look out to sea, thinking about how frenetic the last week had been, when he suddenly became aware of the crowd parting to make way for a large man who was walking towards him. It was Carl Martin Norman Hansen.

'When is that duel to be fought?' said someone in the crowd, and Gibbs felt a sick feeling in his stomach as he readied himself for Norman Hansen to attack. But much to his relief, Norman Hansen laughed and held out a big hand.

'We will fight with the pen and not with the sword,' he said, and they shook hands. The reason for his amiability is unclear. Perhaps he had never intended his article to be interpreted as a challenge to a duel, or maybe Cook's failure to produce his proof had caused his own doubts to resurface.

With Cook now gone, all that was left was for Gibbs to write a last article about his departure, and he used it to look back at his time in Copenhagen and to wonder for a final time about the enigmatic figure who had become his nemesis:

I stood below the gangway watching that extraordinary man, who still smiled, and smiled with that strange fixed baffling smile which he has worn for a week. To me the scene was amazing. I was not surprised that the people cheered him. The Danes are a generous-hearted people, and they have taken this man's word without having had the advantage, if I may say so, of having read the evidence given in the *Daily Chronicle*. But that he should still have the official recognition of scientists and explorers, and, to a certain degree, of the American Minister – although Dr Egan tells me, for publication that he does not in any way guarantee Dr Cook, but gives him the usual courtesy of an American citizen – is a surprising thing, which must not be forgotten when the full history of this affair comes to be written.

For who is this man who stood on the bridge of the Melchior? He is a man who came with an amazing story, demanding instant proof. He is a man who promised to present his proofs. He is a man who has broken that promise, and has not presented his proofs, and has gone away without doing so. I have convicted him of broken pledges, of daily twistings and turnings to avoid this pursuit of evidence, and men as famous as I am unknown have made the most terrible accusations against him, to which he has given no answer at all except denial. This was the man who today stood with a wreath of roses in his hand, smiling and lifting his bowler hat as the vessel warped from the quayside and took him away towards his own country – a man who has left his papers in other hands, though he should rather have parted with life than with them. He has retreated hurriedly from Europe because he has no papers to show to those who have demanded them.

He went on to make a final attack on Cook's credibility, writing about how Cook had already changed his mind about sending an expedition to bring back the Inuit, and disputing his claim that it was now too late in the year to send a ship to Greenland. 'It is not too late,' he wrote, 'as everybody in Copenhagen knows, and as Mr Sverdrup knows, for the *Hans Egede*, which brought Dr Cook to Copenhagen, is going back to Greenland in a week's time. I say, how did he dare to make that statement to the University, raising his hands with that dramatic gesture of solemn oathing?'

Gibbs also recalled showing polar explorers the map of Cook's supposed journey and them telling him it would have been impossible and that 'all this tale is a wild dream'. He repeated Peter Freuchen's argument that Cook could never have carried enough food by sledge. He questioned Cook's claim to have used a canvas boat, ridiculing the idea that a boat made of canvas could have carried him, the Inuit, the dogs and all their provisions (though, as far as I can find, Cook never claimed that it had). And he rubbished the idea that he could have killed 38 muskoxen at Cape Sparbo, citing an explorer who had been to Cape Sparbo who had told him muskoxen would not be able to live in the conditions there.

'It is such facts as these, and so many of them, that destroy Dr Cook's claim,' Gibbs concluded. 'He has not yet produced the proofs of the truthfulness of his story, but I say that he has actually and irretrievably produced the proofs of its falsehood.'

With those words, he finished what was the last *Daily Chronicle* article he would ever write about Cook and the North Pole. He telegraphed it back to London and then visited *Politiken*'s office to hand them a statement responding to Norman Hansen's accusation that he had lied about his interview with Cook. 'Allow me, in reading the article in *Politiken* today, to state that I have never presented my conversation with Dr Cook on board the *Hans Egede* as having taken place on my own,' Gibbs wrote. 'My interview with Dr Cook was watched by several Danish journalists. I am glad it was, because it would have been dangerous to have interviewed Dr Cook without witnesses.'

'I have only one thing to add,' he told the *Politiken* journalist as he handed him his statement, 'that when Dr Norman Hansen challenges me, he need only state which weapon, sword or pistol.' The journalist was evidently impressed – his article about Gibbs's visit was in Danish, but it included three words in English: 'Gibbs is willing.' The journalist may, though, have been less impressed if he had known Norman Hansen had laughed off the idea of a duel earlier that day, or that Gibbs would be about to leave for England by the time *Politiken* published his response to Norman Hansen's challenge.

By that evening, most of the journalists who had descended on Copenhagen had sent back their last articles (W.T. Stead still maintained his belief that 'mistaken he may be … [but] he is both too honest and too limited to have conceived so colossal a fraud') and were on trains out of the city. Gibbs was one of the few foreign correspondents to spend one last night in Copenhagen before heading home. Cook's supporters saw the fact that Gibbs was returning to London rather than following Cook to New York as evidence that the *Daily Chronicle* had lost faith in his objectivity. The *New York Herald* reported that 'it is significant that another correspondent, not Gibbs, is leaving for New York to watch the controversy for the *Daily Chronicle*'.[7] But this does not really add up. Yes, it is true that by this point Gibbs was no longer objectively reporting the story, but neither was the *Daily Chronicle*. With its long editorial accusing Cook of lying, the newspaper had crossed the same Rubicon as Gibbs. The motivation for Gibbs not going to New York is likely to have been more mundane – he had been away from home for over a week after leaving unexpectedly, and his novel, *Street of Adventure*, was about to be published and he may have wanted to be near London for it. And if the *Chronicle* already had a reporter in New York, it would make financial sense to leave the reporting of it to them.

But even if reports that the *Chronicle* had lost faith in Gibbs's reporting were untrue, there were many people who criticised his articles about Cook. While the previous six days had dramatically increased Gibbs's profile – *The Westminster Gazette* reporting that 'Mr Philip Gibbs is much in the public eye just now'[8] and *The Scotsman* commenting that his 'name has recently been prominently before the public'[9] – the jury was still out on whether his attacks had been prescient or reckless. A journalist for Washington DC's *Evening Post* wrote 'this Philip Gibbs person's junk, as he writ it [*sic*] from Copenhagen for his London paper was so laughably raw, so obviously the shyster material of a special pleader (and no very skilful one, at that) engaged in an attempt to make out a case, that it furnished a large and continuous bunch of laughs for the entire civilized world'.[10]

But what the world thought of Gibbs as he sailed back to England on 11 September 1909 was not really the point. As he looked out to sea, he must have realised that over the next few months the world would come to a view on whether Cook was one of the greatest explorers in history or the perpetrator of an audacious fraud. The world's verdict on Cook would also be a verdict on Gibbs. If Cook was a fraud, he would be celebrated for having exposed him. But if Cook really had reached the Pole, his reputation would be ruined. And as the debate on Cook shifted from Copenhagen to New York, so Gibbs's role was about to change from being a protagonist to that of a helpless observer from across the Atlantic.

A portrait of Philip Gibbs that was painted in 1908, the year before he met Frederick Cook in Copenhagen. (Courtesy of the Gibbs family archive)

'Man of unfaltering courage': by the time he left to attempt to reach the Pole, Frederick Cook was one of the most respected explorers in the United States. (From *The World's Work* (New York: May 1909), p.565)

Front-page news: how the *New York Tribune* covered Frederick Cook's polar claim.
(Library of Congress)

Back to civilisation: Frederick Cook arrives at Copenhagen on 4 September 1909. (From J. Martin Miller's (ed.) *Discovery of the North Pole* (Philadelphia: G.A. Parker, 1909), MBLWHOI Library)

One of the biggest lucky breaks in journalism history: Dagmar Rasmussen walks into the Copenhagen café that Gibbs happens to be sitting in. (Drawing commissioned for Philip Gibbs's autobiography, courtesy of the Gibbs family archive)

'Dr Cook, I believe?': Philip Gibbs (left) climbs aboard the *Hans Egede* to meet Frederick Cook (right). (Drawing commissioned for Philip Gibbs's autobiography, courtesy of the Gibbs family archive)

Philip Gibbs interviews Frederick Cook on board the *Hans Egede*. (Drawing commissioned for, but not published in, Philip Gibbs's autobiography, courtesy of the Gibbs family archive)

Home: Frederick Cook is welcomed back to New York on 21 September 1909. (Library of Congress)

'Lion-hearted in courage': Frederick Cook poses in polar clothing in 1911. (Library of Congress)

Hr. Philip Gibbs.

'Murderous-looking portrait': Philip Gibbs would remember the *Politiken* drawing of him for the rest of his life. (Courtesy of *Politiken*, 22 December 1909)

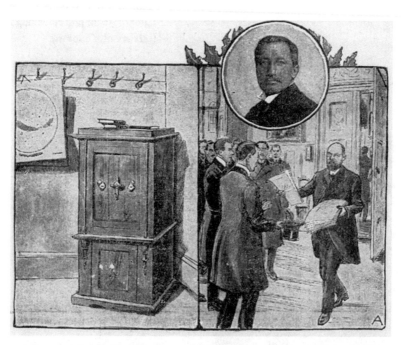

Judgement day: *Politiken*'s drawing of the commission's report being handed to a journalist, and of the cabinet where Frederick Cook's papers were stored. (Courtesy of *Politiken*, 22 December 1909)

Three polar stars: Roald Amundsen, Ernest Shackleton, and Robert Peary in 1913. (National Library of Norway)

Arctic explorer Peter Freuchen, who helped Philip Gibbs during his time in Copenhagen. (Magite Historic/Alamy Stock Photo)

A young Knud Rasmussen, one of the world's leading experts on Inuit culture and one of the last people to see Cook before his dash for the Pole. (Library of Congress)

Arctic explorer Otto Sverdrup (right), who befriended Cook and disliked Peary, alongside former 'farthest north' record holder Fridtjof Nansen (left). (National Library of Norway)

The rival for the Pole: Robert Peary in 1909. (Peary-MacMillan Arctic Museum, Bowdoin College)

Philip Gibbs as one of the accredited correspondents in France during the First World War. (Courtesy of the Gibbs family archive)

12

WE BELIEVE IN YOU

Frederick Cook reached Kristiansand in Norway just as Gibbs was heading home to England. As the *Melchior* arrived there, he was saluted by seven guns fired from its fort by order of King Haakon VII, the younger brother of Denmark's Crown Prince Christian, and then Cook transferred to the steamer that was to take him to New York.

During the ten-day voyage, Cook spent time walking on the deck and managed to catch up on his sleep. Before leaving Copenhagen, he had agreed to write a detailed account of his expedition for the *New York Herald* for the huge fee of $25,000, and he must have worked on it during the crossing because the *Herald* started publishing instalments as soon as the steamer got within wireless range, near Newfoundland.

As the steamer made its way across the Atlantic, Peary kept up his attack on Cook. 'It is simply untrue,' he replied to a journalist who asked him about Cook's polar claim. 'I am the only man who ever reached the North Pole. I am prepared to prove it … Dr Cook did not reach the Pole, and I have concrete proof in support of that statement … I intend to wait until Dr Cook issues a statement, and then I shall make public the information I have, upon which the scientific bodies will pass judgement. Then nothing will be left of Dr Cook's statement.'[1]

Just before Cook arrived in New York, he telegraphed his response: 'To Peary, the explorer, I am still willing to tip my hat, but Peary's unfounded accusations have disclosed another side to his character which will never be forgotten.'[2]

Cook expected a relatively quiet arrival in New York, believing his home city was 'too big, too unemotional, too much interested in bigger matters to bother much about the North Pole'.[3] But he failed to grasp how much his story had captured the American imagination over the previous three weeks: within days of the news, sweet shops were selling 'Cook gumdrops', a Cook cocktail was drunk on Broadway – lemon juice, gin, egg white, and cherry liqueur – and a Chicago store advertised Cook-themed fur hats. Whatever doubts now existed around his polar claim, the welcome awaiting him in New York on 21 September 1909 was almost as wild and ecstatic as Copenhagen's had been.

Before he reached shore, a tug carrying his family came alongside his steamer and he jumped down onto it from a rope ladder and ran to embrace Marie and their two children. After they spent half an hour together quietly as a family, the tug made the short distance to a Brooklyn pier, where a woman put a wreath of white flowers around Cook's neck and the crowd surged onto the boat and hoisted him onto its shoulders.

When Cook was finally able to step onto the pier, a cordon of 100 police officers formed around him but the crowd was so thick that it took him ten minutes to make it the 50ft distance to a waiting car. The car drove him into the city at the head of a convoy of 200 cars, a remarkable spectacle in an age when cars were still relatively uncommon. The convoy made its way through crowd-lined streets, with people standing on roofs to see him.[4] As his car passed his former home in Brooklyn, Cook was amazed to see a huge wooden arch had been constructed over the road in his honour. At its centre was a picture of him, along with the words, 'We believe in you'. Four white pigeons were released as Cook's car passed under the arch.

He was driven to the Bushwick Club in Brooklyn, where he acknowledged the crowd from the balcony and then attended a large reception before dining with dignitaries in the club's banquet room, a band and a choir serenading him from the street below as he ate.

New York's journalists, like the journalists in Copenhagen, struggled to find the words to adequately describe both the hysteria of the crowd and Cook's unusual personality. The *New York World* correspondent was as fascinated by the curious look in Cook's eyes as Gibbs had been: 'The crowds roared and stamped, whistles blew and horns honked and several times the doctor was almost swept off his feet, but he showed no great joy or pride. Behind his dancing blue eyes of shallow depth there lies either wonderful power of self-control or an innate insensibility to the ordinary emotions.'[5]

The next day, Cook met a group of around 40 journalists. *The Times* reported that he 'cheerfully answered all pertinent questions' and that his 'answers came unhesitatingly' despite him being subjected to a 'severe cross-examination'. When one of the journalists asked to see his records, he left the room for a few minutes and returned with a notebook filled with his handwriting. He said it was one of three notebooks containing the story of his trip to the Pole, and the realisation that they were the first people to see what was apparently evidence to support his claim sent a frisson of excitement through the gathering.

Cook told the journalists it would take about two months for him to produce his records and data, and that he would present them to the University of Copenhagen in recognition of Denmark's warm welcome of him and the fact that the university had already awarded him an honorary degree.[6] The *Daily Chronicle* correspondent thought this seemed just another stalling tactic, and he asked Cook why he could not have done this while he was in Copenhagen. Cook looked at him with what the reporter thought was an enigmatic smile. 'I can afford to wait,' he said.

'As a matter of fact, he can afford to wait,' the journalist wrote in his article about the press conference, 'for Americans generally seem content with the knowledge that the discovery of the Pole is, in any case, a national achievement, and they are also prepared to bide their time and await the outcome of the dispute.'[7]

The next day, the Waldorf Astoria hotel hosted a banquet for more than 1,000 people in Cook's honour. In a room decorated with

American flags and with a plaster bust of Cook in the middle,[8] Cook was introduced by Admiral Winfield Scott Schley, the Spanish–American war hero Cook had quoted when he first learned of Peary's polar claim. The diners rose to their feet and cheered him as the orchestra played 'Hail to the Chief' and 'He's a Jolly Good Fellow'. Admiral Schley told the diners: 'Like all men who have achieved similar success in other fields of activity, he is challenged by those who doubt his word ... That often happens after disappointment on the part of those who have failed in an undertaking. All fair-minded people believe Dr Cook and refuse to see any issue brought up to dim the glory of his achievement. It is envy that produces a challenge of this sort, in most instances.'

Cook fiddled with his glass as he listened to the applause, and then gave a short speech thanking them for their welcome and, generous spirited as always, he emphasised the efforts of those who had been the 'stepping stones to ultimate success'. It was not unusual for an explorer to acknowledge his predecessors' achievements, but Cook also took care to praise the contribution of Native Americans and the Inuit, saying that without their knowledge of pemmican, snowshoes, and the use of dogs, he would never have reached the Pole. 'To savage man, therefore, who has no flag, we are bound to give a part of this fruit,' he said. After dinner, he attended a reception where he shook hands with more than 2,000 people, afterwards telling Arctic Club officials that 'my hand is a little sore but otherwise I have never felt better in my life'.[9]

But as dazzling as New York's welcome had been, the convoy through crowd-lined streets and the grandeur of the banquet would soon seem less the triumphant return of one of the heroes of the age and more a high-water mark for Cook's reputation. Four days after the banquet, he received disturbing news from Harry Whitney, the big game hunter he said he had given his instruments to. Whitney reportedly told him he was getting a lift back on Peary's boat, but that Peary had refused to let him take anything belonging to Cook on board, and so Whitney had left Cook's instruments in a cache in Greenland.

Cook later remembered 'my dismay, my heartsickness'[10] at hearing the news, and as he walked through a park with his family he was assailed by reporters asking for his reaction. Had he not previously said the instruments would be vital for corroborating his story, they asked him. Cook stared into space as he thought about how to respond. 'I had counted on him bringing the instruments and everything with him,' he said, finally. 'Naturally, I am disappointed.'[11]

The day after Whitney's message, Cook gave a lecture to 2,500 people at Carnegie Hall, and then travelled to Philadelphia to give another lecture, a crowd of thousands welcoming him to the city. He then went on to lecture in Washington DC, where he stood on the back seat of a car and doffed his hat at crowds lining Pennsylvania Avenue. There were more big crowds for lectures in Pittsburgh, St Louis, Kansas City, Ann Arbor, Detroit, Chicago, Cleveland, and Buffalo. His lecture tour was astonishingly lucrative: for his lecture in St Louis alone, he was reportedly paid $10,000. But the lectures involved constant travel, and left him struggling to find the time and space to think about how to respond to Peary's attacks and what to do now that Whitney had left his instruments in Greenland.

Peary's campaign against him was proving to be as aggressive and single-minded as Peary himself, but for the first few weeks after Cook arrived in New York it consisted of not much more than ominous threats. Then on 13 October, the Peary Arctic Club produced what it said was proof of Cook's fraud – a statement from the members of Peary's expedition and a map of Cook's expedition, which it claimed was based on Inuit testimony, that showed Cook had not got anywhere near the Pole.

The *Daily Chronicle* seized on the news as the final word on Cook's claim. Under the front-page headline 'The *Daily Chronicle*'s position vindicated', it concluded: 'It is scarcely credible, after the publication of the evidence which we are now able to place before our readers, that there can longer exist reasonable doubt in anyone's mind of the absurdity of Dr Cook's claim to have reached the North Pole ... These crushing documents now published ought finally to dispose of any remnants of Dr Cook's reputation, and even the faithful citizens of Brooklyn must feel some qualms concerning their hero.'

The *Chronicle* was clearly looking for anything that supported its view that Cook was lying. But for others, a map and a statement that was nothing more than hearsay was an anti-climax after Peary's promise to produce incontrovertible proof. If anything, it seems to have done more to reinforce a sense of revulsion at Peary's ungentlemanly conduct than to increase doubt in Cook's story. The *Chicago Journal*, for example, thought 'Commander Peary's bombastic bulletins have destroyed confidence in his reputed triumph',[12] and the *New York Tribune* called his attacks 'neither sportsmanlike, scientific nor ethical'.[13] Newspapers also accused Peary of behaving disgracefully in refusing to let Whitney bring Cook's equipment onto his ship, seeing his refusal as evidence that he must have believed Cook might have reached the Pole. And polls showed that the public thought Cook had a better claim to the Pole than Peary, with Cook's humility and willingness to share credit standing in increasingly stark contrast to Peary's aggression.

But then came much more damaging news. When newspapers had previously questioned Cook's claim to have climbed Mount McKinley in 1906, the one person he had said was with him when he reached the top, Ed Barrill, had remained silent, telling journalists he would wait until Cook was back in the United States. Now, *The New York Globe* reported that Barrill had signed a sworn affidavit alleging Cook's claim to have reached the summit had been a calculated fraud.

In his affidavit, Barrill swore he had been with Cook throughout the expedition and that they had not got within 14 miles of the top and had only reached an elevation roughly half the height of the mountain. He claimed Cook had ordered him to write fraudulent diary entries, and that a photograph of Barrill that Cook said was taken at the summit had actually been taken at a much lower point. 'The doctor took the American flag out of one of the bags and handed it to me, and sent me back to the top of the point, and told me to hold it there on the end of the ice axe, which I did,' the affidavit went on. 'The doctor then with his camera took the picture … I then came down with the flag to where Dr Cook was standing with his camera, and I made the remark that the eight peaks on the other side of the point where I had been photographed would probably show in the picture, and he said that he had taken the picture at such an angle that those peaks would not show … He stated to me as follows: "That point would make a good top for Mount McKinley."'[14]

The owner of *The New York Globe* was General Thomas Hubbard, who was so close to Peary that he was president of the Peary Arctic Club, and alongside its publication of the affidavit the *Globe* gloated that Cook's claim now lay 'smashed'. 'To those of sanity,' it argued, 'the Mount McKinley revelation means the exit of Cook, the intrepid explorer, and the entry of Cook as one who has chosen a queer road to immortality.' In Britain, the *Daily Chronicle* agreed, calling the Barrill affidavit 'another scathing indictment'.[15]

Cook was in Atlantic City when the *Globe* published Barrill's affidavit, and he was shown it by a group of journalists. He read it in front of them and then calmly said he had not even known Barrill had kept an expedition diary, so could not have asked him to alter it. Whether or not they were convinced by him, the reporters were impressed by his coolness under pressure. 'As usual, he never once lost his self-control,' wrote one of them. 'There was no sign of anger in his expression, and he talked straight into the eyes of his questioners.'[16]

After he had time to think, Cook gave an interview to the Associated Press, telling them he was shocked Barrill had sworn to such a statement and that he believed he had been paid to do so, seeing it as significant that it had appeared in a newspaper so closely connected to Peary. Cook had guessed correctly. Barrill was almost certainly paid thousands of dollars, a huge sum of money at the time, to sign the affidavit, and General Hubbard had timed its publication to cause Cook maximum damage – the day before Cook was due to become only the fourth person, and the first ever American, to be given the freedom of New York.

Barrill's affidavit was not without its problems. He was claiming to have spent the previous three years lying about having reached the top of McKinley, and yet was now asking the public to believe he was telling the truth. Yet for all the reasons to dismiss the story as black propaganda, the level of detail in the affidavit gave it a ring of truth, and Barrill's version of events was supported by what other members of the McKinley expedition had told newspapers.

Hubbard hoped the affidavit would force the Aldermen of New York to cancel or postpone giving Cook the Freedom of the City, but they decided to go ahead with the ceremony. It meant that, for the second time in barely a month, an august body was presenting Cook with a prestigious honour just as newspapers were making serious allegations about his honesty.

'This is the proudest moment of my life,' Cook said, as he accepted the honour. 'To feel that you have confidence in me amidst the unfounded statements and against the false affidavits published during the last few days, creates a feeling of pride in me – worthy pride in the knowledge that my countrymen believe my word. I will substantiate every claim I have made with every proof within the power of man, and believe me, ladies and gentlemen, when I say that this tribute paid me today will never be misplaced.'[17]

Cook realised the credibility of his polar claim rested on him being able to discredit Barrill, and he issued a statement claiming prominent citizens in Barrill's hometown of Hamilton, Montana, were prepared to confirm Barrill had spent the previous three years saying he had climbed McKinley. But when *The New York Times*, by this point clearly supporting Peary over Cook, sent a message to the town to ask the general opinion there, the president of its chamber of commerce replied that Barrill had repeatedly admitted to 'reputable citizens' that he and Cook had not reached the top. *The New York Times* sent a reporter to the Waldorf Astoria, where Cook was staying, to show him the message. Cook slowly read it and handed it back to the reporter. 'I have no comment to make,' he said.[18] The same day, *The New York Times* reported that the McKinley expedition's cook, assistant guide, and photographer had all signed affidavits casting doubt on whether Cook had reached the top.[19] It was beginning to feel like his claim to have climbed McKinley, which had been the foundation of credibility his North Pole claim had been built on, was crumbling.

The evening after being awarded the Freedom of the City, Cook arrived back at the Waldorf Astoria to find a group of journalists in the reception hall. 'I want to say to you gentlemen that I shall have nothing to say about Mount McKinley,' he said, standing with his hands in his pockets. 'That whole matter is now in the hands of my lawyer.' But apparently incapable of appearing in front of a group of journalists without announcing some news to them, he then added that he would prove he had reached the top. 'I shall organise an expedition of my own that will make a trip to Mount McKinley,' he said. 'I shall lead the expedition over precisely the same course followed by my last expedition. I expect I shall find there the records I left.'

As well as announcing a new expedition to McKinley, Cook decided to cut short his lecture tour. Cancelling his lectures meant giving up a reported $100,000 in fees, but he wanted to give himself enough time to concentrate on preparing his records for the University of Copenhagen. But first, he gave another couple of paid lectures and then decided to take the fight to the enemy by giving a free lecture in Barrill's hometown, apparently hoping to meet people there who would con-firm Barrill had told them he had reached the top of McKinley. But his lecture in Hamilton, Montana, was a disaster. Both Barrill and expedition guide Fred Printz were there, and members of the audience shouted insults at Cook as he tried to talk. Then when Cook said Barrill was lying, Barrill got up onto the stage and demanded the chance to respond. Cook did not want to share the stage with him, and so he walked off the back of it. But on leaving the stage, he saw there was no exit at the back of the building, and the only way to leave would have been to go back onto the stage and out through the audience. For an excruciating half hour, Cook stood behind the stage, refusing to come back out until, realising he had no choice, he reluctantly returned to the stage. 'Beads of sweat stood out on his forehead, and it was plainly evident that he would rather have been anywhere else than in Hamilton just then,' wrote a journalist who was there.

There followed an awkward scene where Cook and Barrill stood together on stage, both looking uncomfortable as they accused each other of lying. Then someone pointed out that Barrill was the only one of them who had signed an affidavit, and Cook called for a pen and paper and wrote out his own statement swearing that he and Barrill really had reached the summit, and signed his name under it. Then, in a final humiliation, the meeting passed a motion affirming its trust in Barrill and Printz, in doing so saying it thought Cook was lying.

'Disgusted, with a heavy heart, I left the hall,' Cook wrote. 'The oppression of my loneliness, defencelessness, and hopeless confusion rendered all sleep impossible that night ... The net result of this experience was the conviction in my own mind that I was regarded everywhere, throughout the entire country, as a liar.'[20]

The lecture led to yet more negative newspaper coverage. But with his lecture commitments at an end, Cook was at least now finally able to throw himself into preparing his papers. He quietly booked into a hotel in Bronxville, a small village north of New York City, and after a month working on his submission he gave a package of material to his secretary, a man named Walter Lonsdale, who Maurice Egan had recommended to him. Lonsdale boarded a steamer to Copenhagen, where he was to present the materials to a commission of Arctic experts assembled by the university. The stress of the last few months had clearly taken its toll on Cook. 'When I saw him last week for some moments he seemed to have aged ten years in a few months, and was undoubtedly suffering,' the *Daily Telegraph & Courier* correspondent wrote.[21] With his papers on their way across the Atlantic, Cook now disappeared from public view.

With Cook's whereabouts unknown, it was left to his lawyer, H. Wellington Wack, to speak on his behalf. Wack immediately caused yet more controversy by making the extraordinary claim that the Cook camp had uncovered a plot to drug Lonsdale en route to Copenhagen and steal Cook's records. Because of this, Wack claimed, Lonsdale was carrying a dummy package and Cook's real proofs were on their way to Denmark via a secret route. It was a bizarre allegation that had more than a whiff of paranoia about it, and it added to a growing impression that Cook's judgement was lacking.

Lonsdale arrived in Copenhagen on 8 December 1909, going straight to a bank to deposit a small box there and then meeting with officials at the university. Then the next day, *The New York Times* published perhaps the most damaging allegation Cook had faced since he had arrived in Copenhagen three months earlier. In what it called the 'most extraordinary instalment of the whole Cook epic of polar exploration', it made the incendiary claim that Cook had hired a Norwegian navigator called August Wedel Loose to produce a series of observations that could be used as evidence to support his North Pole claim. Loose and his representative, a man named George Dunkle, had signed affidavits claiming Loose had worked on the observations while staying under a false name at the same Bronxville hotel as Cook, and that they had been promised $4,000 for their services, along with another $500 if the University of Copenhagen's judgement went in Cook's favour. Loose and Dunkle apparently felt betrayed when Cook disappeared after paying them only $260, and so had taken their revenge by going to the press.

As with Barrill's claim that he had previously been lying about the McKinley expedition, Loose and Dunkle's apparent lack of integrity in agreeing to create the observations in the first place raised questions about how much they could be trusted now. But *New York Times* reporters had checked some of the details and found the false name that Loose said he had used in the hotel register for the dates he said he had stayed there, and hotel staff told them they remembered Loose asking for Cook at the reception desk. The two men also gave *The New York Times* the observations Loose had prepared for Cook and, damningly, a note that seemed to be in Cook's handwriting, setting out the observations he needed.

This suggested Cook had planned to submit fraudulent evidence to the University of Copenhagen, but it did not necessarily mean he was lying about reaching the Pole. Even if Loose and Dunkle were telling the truth, it was plausible Cook might have decided to use fake observations because Harry Whitney had left the real ones in Greenland. But Loose, an experienced navigator, was convinced Cook had not reached the Pole. 'It took me only about three minutes on my first acquaintance with Dr Cook to get the idea into my head that he had never found the North Pole,' Loose wrote. 'I found that he was entirely ignorant on many vital points of method of taking observations ... I could not help wondering how he ever imagined he had found the Pole if he did not know how to take observations. The idea forced itself upon me that he had just imagined it.'

With Cook uncontactable, it fell to Lonsdale in Copenhagen to respond to the story. He accused Dunkle and Loose of being 'slanderers', telling journalists that Cook had only hired Loose to help him with a 'general rehearsal' before he sent his records to Copenhagen. He added that Cook had neither showed Loose his original records nor used his observations in his evidence to the university, and that he had fired him after he had suffered a 'relapse into intemperance'. Lonsdale hoped his comments would help Cook by minimising Loose and Dunkle's involvement, but journalists in Copenhagen thought Lonsdale's confirmation that Cook had engaged with these dubious characters was even more shocking than the original *New York Times* article about the affidavits. At best, it was evidence of scarcely conceivable naivety; at worst, it seemed like the smoking gun that finally proved Cook had been lying all along.[22]

But just as the Loose and Dunkle affidavits seemed to have dealt a potentially fatal blow to Cook's credibility, there was some good news for him. Knud Rasmussen, whose view of Cook's claim had been the subject of so much speculation, was now back in Copenhagen and gave a lecture in which he said he still believed in Cook and urged people to wait for the University of Copenhagen's verdict before making up their minds.[23]

Then, four days later, Rasmussen was called to give his views to the six experts who formed the University of Copenhagen commission that now gathered in a small brick building at the university.[24] The task before them was to examine Cook's records and answer the question the whole world was asking: did Cook's submission constitute proof that he was the first person in the history of humanity to have set foot on the top of the world?

13

HIS OWN FOOLISH ACTS

The University of Copenhagen had not given a date by which its commission of experts was expected to reach a conclusion about Cook's polar claim, but the complexity of the issue meant most observers expected it to take some time. So it was a surprise when just four days after they first convened, on Monday, 21 December 1909, an article in that morning's *Politiken* speculated that the commission was about to publish its report, and that its findings were unlikely to be good news for Cook.

Just after 1 p.m. that day, journalists were called into a room at the university and handed copies of the commission's report. It soon became clear why the experts had been able to produce it so quickly — the evidence presented to them had been so meagre that there had been little of substance for them to deliberate on. Rather than the detailed observations they had been expecting, the commission members were shocked to discover that the box Walter Lonsdale had carried across the Atlantic contained nothing more than a report by Lonsdale that essentially repeated Cook's *New York Herald* account, and 16 typewritten pages that had apparently been copied from one of Cook's notebooks. Lonsdale told the committee that Cook had sent his original notebooks via another route and that they would be arriving in Copenhagen shortly. Cook had not even included a covering letter, and the committee was told it had no way of contacting him. Even Lonsdale did not know where he was.

Over the previous three months, Cook had repeatedly promised that everything would be settled once he was finally ready to produce his proofs. But on the first day the commission met, it agreed that Cook's papers were, in the words of its report, 'completely valueless for the determination of the question, whether Dr Cook had reached the North Pole'. The only real data they included were some pedometer readings that corresponded with the distance Cook claimed to have travelled. But these only added to the commission's suspicions because the ice would have been drifting and so the pedometer reading would be extremely unlikely to exactly match the distance he travelled. The commission's chairman, Professor Elis Strömgren, who three months earlier had reportedly told journalists that 'there is no reason for any shadow of doubt as to the fact that he reached the Pole', decided there was so little evidence that there was no point extending the discussion into a second day. Instead, he called a meeting for the following day for the commission to write its report.

Lonsdale was invited to this meeting, and he presented the commission with a letter from Cook that had been stamped in Marseilles three days earlier. 'After many wakeful nights, I have come to the conclusion that it is unfair to the Danes to ask them to accept our incomplete record – as a final proof of the conquest,' Cook had written. 'I prefer to submit the digest which you have as a preliminary report asking the university to forgo the final examination until the things are brought from Greenland.' Cook had also enclosed a letter he had written to Professor Carl Torp at the end of September but never sent, in which he explained that Peary's refusal to let Whitney take Cook's equipment onto his ship meant that 'part of the records and instruments which are now necessary to prove my case are buried among the rocks at Etah', and so 'without the instruments and the entire series of original field notes it seems unwise and impossible to submit for final examination the present report'.

Cook's letter and Lonsdale's explanation only raised more questions. If Cook had known at the end of September that he would not be able to produce proof, why was he only telling the university now? If he knew this then, what had he been doing at the hotel in Bronxville and why had he hired Dunkle and Loose? And what about the proof Lonsdale had said was on its way to Copenhagen by another route but of which there was still no sign? There were no obvious answers to these questions, and of Cook, the one person who might have been able to attempt to answer them, the only thing anyone knew about his whereabouts was that he appeared to have been in France three days earlier.

We can only imagine the commission members' dismay as they discussed the paltry evidence before them, and how this dismay must have turned to cold fury in the face of Lonsdale's and Cook's weak and confusing explanations. They may have also felt a sense of regret and embarrassment as they thought back to the speed with which the university had awarded Cook his honorary degree in September. The report they wrote that afternoon was couched in the formal and measured language of an official document, but the formality did little to hide the authors' sense of anger and betrayal: 'There is in the documents submitted to us a not permissible lack of such guiding information which could show the probability that the mentioned astronomical observations had actually been undertaken. Neither had the more practical side of the question – the sleigh trip – been described by such details which could help to control the report. The Commission is therefore of the opinion that there cannot in the material which has been submitted to us for examination, be found any proof whatsoever of Dr Cook having reached the North Pole.'

In concluding that Cook had not provided any evidence that he had reached the Pole, the commission stopped short of accusing him of not having reached it. Cook would later seize on this by claiming that 'the verdict on this was that in such material there was no absolute proof of the attainment of the Pole',[1] and arguing that it was a 'neutral verdict which carried no implication of the non-attainment of the Pole'.[2] But the report's wording left no doubt that the commission was at the very least highly sceptical. Given it followed a long series of reasons to doubt Cook, it was immediately accepted by almost everybody as the

His Own Foolish Acts

final word on his claim. For all the previous controversies, from Gibbs's articles to Peary's attacks, Cook's response had been to urge his doubters to wait until his evidence had been judged by a group of scientists. That had now happened, and the group of scientists had concluded there was no evidence to support his claim.

If the report's formal wording meant it pulled its punches, the individual commission members made their feelings absolutely clear when they spoke to journalists. 'The most flattering opinion expressed of him is that he was an incredibly stupid bungler,' wrote *The New York Times*'s correspondent. 'The theory which at one time obtained among some of those who doubted Cook's claims, that he was suffering from a hallucination, is no longer held by a single member of the commission which examined the so-called proofs.'[3]

One of the commission members was Gustav Frederik Holm, an Arctic explorer who Holm Land in northern Greenland is named after, and a journalist asked him if it was now established that Cook had not been to the Pole. Holm agreed this was fair. The journalist asked if Cook should now be considered an imposter, and at first Holm refused to answer, cautious about going beyond the conclusion of the commission.

'What is your private opinion?' the journalist pressed him.

'Yes, I now consider him an imposter,' Holm replied.[4]

Holm also gave a longer interview to *Politiken*, in which he was more cautious about accusing Cook of deliberate fraud, but equally firm in his belief that he had not reached the Pole: 'Whether he is a deliberate swindler, I do not know. But he is a swindler. The commission was clear as soon as we had embarked on the investigation. There was no disagreement about that. There were no observations at all. Had there been any, we could probably have caught him on them. But there were none. What do you think the teacher would say if the student at an examination only handed in the result and did not give the calculations? He would simply give him zero. And we have done the same.'

The journalist asked Holm if Cook had included Loose's observations in his submission.

'No, if he had done then we would at least have had something to work on. He has apparently become frightened and dismissed Loose without using his observations.'

But why did Holm think Cook had sent his evidence to the commission, given how little it contained?

'I have no idea. He can hardly have thought we would approve it. Maybe he sent it to get a fortnight's respite in which he could disappear. This is at least a conceivable hypothesis. But, of course, I cannot comment on that.'

Elis Strömgren told journalists that Cook's treatment of the university had been 'shameless'. As chair of the commission and having been publicly accused by Gibbs of naivety for previously accepting Cook's claims at face value, Strömgren must have found the verdict particularly difficult. After speaking to the assembled journalists, he invited the *Politiken* correspondent into the commission's room, opened the safe deposit box and took out the two documents Cook had sent them. 'This is the report, but there are no observations in it at all,' Strömgren told him. 'There is not a single astronomical observation in this booklet, just remarks on weather and wind and ice and snow, which could be excellent to supplement, but that's not proof. And someone who does not have observations cannot prove he has been to the North Pole. Dr Cook is not truthful. We telegraphed him in October to ask when he would send his instruments and original observations, and he replied that his instruments were in Etah, but that the records were to come. And then he sends us nothing.'

Strömgren said he realised Cook had not been to the Pole as soon as he saw his evidence, and the journalist asked Strömgren why he had previously been so quick to believe him. 'I had no reason to doubt him,' he replied. 'The attacks on him were both indecent and ill-founded. Any questions I immediately had when Dr Cook was in the city, he answered immediately. He answered briefly, precisely, to exactly what was being asked. Presumably it was out of wisdom that he never said more than he needed to. Later, I was able to establish that some of the information he gave me at the time was incorrect. But I could not see that then. For example, the number of observations he claimed to have made at the North Pole is contradicted by what he wrote in his report in the *New York Herald*. One of the statements, then, is untrue.'

The journalist asked him if the commission had considered Loose's and Dunkle's claims in coming to its decision.

'We kept it out until the decision was made. Later, I read it, and it is certainly very interesting in several respects.' Strömgren pointed at Cook's documents on the table. 'More interesting than these papers,' he said, wryly.

Knud Rasmussen was also approached by journalists. Ten days earlier, he had still believed in Cook, but now his name was included along with the six commission members as one of the report authors. He told *Politiken*:

I have been in favour of the doctor, and so it will perhaps astonish the public that I have signed a declaration that goes so strongly against him. But I know more now than I knew at the time when I sent my report from Greenland. The fact that the original notebooks were not included immediately aroused our suspicion. Then when we came to the report, this turned into certainty.

None of us took the report seriously for a moment – it was clear to all of us that either the doctor was a swindler or a very simple person. Such a pathetic submission has probably never before been submitted to a scientific society for investigation. The report itself, as well as the transcript of the diaries, contained nothing beyond what has already been published in the *New York Herald*. On some points it did not even contain that much, as the parts of the *New York Herald* account that had provoked the strongest criticism were completely omitted. The story was astonishingly poor in details that could shed light and inspire confidence. The report lacks explanations on the crucial points. It is full of holes. Dr Cook is a man who has abilities as an Arctic explorer. His sleigh ride from Cape Sparbo to Etah is something that deserves respect, and it was this that led me to trust his word. Now, I must say with regret that since I became acquainted with Dr Cook's material, I have completely lost faith in his claim to be the discoverer of the North Pole.

Rasmussen also spoke to the *New York Times* correspondent. 'The papers which Cook sent to Copenhagen University are most impudent,' he told him. 'No schoolboy could make such calculations. It is a most childish attempt at cheating. Cook has killed himself by his own foolish acts.'[5]

Even Walter Lonsdale now seemed unsure if he still believed in Cook. 'My position in this matter is delicate,' he told a *Politiken* journalist. 'I have always believed in Dr Cook, and it is difficult for me to take a new stand. I can only state that the Doctor's behaviour towards me has never given me reason to regard him as anything other than a gentleman.'

Within half an hour of journalists being handed the commission's report, the news was being distributed in the street in Copenhagen on hastily printed sheets of paper. When all the sheets had gone, a crowd gathered around a blackboard with the news on it. The Danish public was suddenly gripped by anger at how Cook seemed to have made fools of them in front of the world, and embarrassment at the hastiness with which their institutions had honoured him.

Ole Olufsen, the Danish explorer who was secretary of the Royal Danish Geographical Society that had awarded Cook its gold medal, called the commission's verdict 'the saddest event of my life'. *Politiken* published a sheepish editorial admitting to feeling 'a crippling astonishment that a man has dared to send a university such worthless scrap', before going on to offer a defence of Denmark's institutions that was really a thinly veiled attempt to justify its own lack of curiosity: 'If Denmark had challenged Dr Cook's account, this attitude would immediately have expressed a distrust for which there was not the remotest reason. That is why authorities and official institutions acted as they did and, we might add, with the full support of public opinion throughout Europe. We in Denmark can at least find solace in the fact that we were only deceived because we believed a man's words. And we can also take comfort in the fact that almost the whole of Europe and a large part of America shared our delusion ... There is at least a justice in the fact it is now from Copenhagen that the judgement comes upon him.'

Politiken published an article by Peter Freuchen, in which he reminded its readers that, in the face of almost universal support for Cook among the Danish people, 'for me there was too much improbability and exaggeration in it'. It also reprinted the sinister-looking drawing of Philip Gibbs that had so irritated him in September. But this time, it was printed under the headline, 'I was the first to call Dr. Cook a swindler'. 'While the levels of enthusiasm were high,' *Politiken* acknowledged, 'Mr Philip Gibbs sent long daily telegrams to his newspaper, asserting that Dr Cook had not convinced him and that he would not be confident the American doctor had reached the Pole until he had the evidence of it in his hand. We interviewed him at the time, and he spoke sharply against Dr Cook. This was not very popular – he had to hear many harsh words among his colleagues in the press, especially from William Stead.'

Just as journalists had sought out the reactions of the world's leading explorers when Cook had first announced he had reached the Pole, so they now asked them for their response to the report that seemed to spell the end for his claim. 'I prefer to believe that Dr Cook himself was confident that he had arrived at the North Pole,' Roald Amundsen told them sadly. 'If he is swindling he must have changed his character in the past 10 years.' Georges Lecointe, who had been with Cook and Amundsen on the *Belgica* and was now scientific director of the Royal Observatory of Belgium, said 'how painful I feel what has arrived to Dr Cook', before adding hopefully that 'perhaps he will furnish some complementary proofs of his declarations; I do wish sincerely but I dare not believe strongly in it'.[6]

Robert Falcon Scott said he had never believed Cook's story but 'wouldn't like to kick a man when he was down'; Ernest Shackleton declined to comment; and former 'farthest north' record holder Fridtjof Nansen thought Cook 'ought to vanish from the consideration of the world'. Just about the only explorer who still held onto the belief that Cook might have reached the Pole was Otto Sverdrup, who later told journalists that 'my faith in Cook is shaken, but not necessarily shattered'.[7] As for Robert Peary, he saw the university's verdict as vindication, providing final proof that not only had he been right about Cook all along, but that it was he who was the real discoverer of the North Pole. He confined his comments to a short statement, presumably wanting to avoid appearing excessively celebratory: 'Three months ago, from the Labrador Coast, I sounded an explicit and deliberately worded warning to the world, based upon complete and accurate information in regards to the Cook claims. In doing so I accepted the responsibility devolving upon me and fulfilled my duty to myself and to the world.'

Herschel Parker, the physicist who had first questioned Cook's McKinley claim in 1906, also spoke to journalists. 'He has made himself and his friends and the American people ridiculous,' he said. 'I don't think Cook will ever be heard of again. I think he has left the country and will never show himself among any of his former associates … In spite of the victory for truth and science I feel a personal regret at Dr Cook's action, both in this and the Mount McKinley matter. He is a most delightful man personally. He should have confined himself to the writing of fiction. At that he is superb.'

In New York, newspapers were merciless in condemning the explorer who had brought shame on their city. *The New York Times* estimated that Cook had earned $100,000 from the deception and suggested the last few months had been nothing more than a cynical attempt to make as much money as possible before his inevitable exposure. 'If the Great Hoax goes down to history in any detailed form,' it concluded, 'probably the most interesting thing about it to historical students will be the perfectly calm way in which its hero brushed aside with a genial smile and a ready explanation the most damaging and crushing disclosures up to the very moment of the final crash.' The *New York Tribune* thought that if Cook 'is not the victim of a monstrous delusion, he is the author of a monstrous fraud'.[8]

In London, the *Daily News* reported that 'Dr Cook, if it does not happily turn out that he has been suffering under hallucination, has played a mean but far-seeing game, and has netted all the advantage that he could reasonably have hoped for'.[9] *Reynold's News* emphasised that 'the verdict of "not proven" is in this case almost as crushing as the verdict of "guilty"';[10] the *Weekly Dispatch* called the report 'the finishing stroke ... to Dr Cook's pretensions to have discovered the North Pole';[11] and *The Times* thought Cook's claim seemed 'to be one of the most audacious attempts upon record to obtain fame by false pretences'. 'The absence of ... evidence was generously attributed to the circumstances in which the announcement of the alleged discovery was made,' it went on. 'Dr Cook explained that his records would be forthcoming in due course, and many men of science, as well as the world in general, saw no reason to disbelieve him. There were, however, sceptics as to the truth of his assertions almost from the beginning, and events have proved that they were more prudent than the individuals, and the public bodies, who precipitately accepted his assertions without the necessary reserve.'[12]

The Times did not mention these sceptics by name, but there were few who had doubted Cook earlier or more loudly than Philip Gibbs and the *Daily Chronicle*. As such, the *Chronicle* was entitled to bask in having been proved right. Under the headline 'Denmark endorses our exposure', it reported the news: 'This damaging verdict will not surprise the readers of the *Daily Chronicle*, whose Special Correspondent during Dr Cook's stay in this city completely exposed the pretensions of the Arctic explorer. In adopting this attitude he stood almost alone. Nearly everybody here, including the whole Press, believed in Dr Cook not wisely but too well, and, it was considered almost a crime to doubt the explorer's veracity.'[13]

The *Chronicle*'s editorial pages went on to scornfully criticise the University of Copenhagen for having been so easily taken in, comparing it to the court in *Alice in Wonderland*. 'It is on the whole the better plan to inquire first, and deliver judgement afterwards,' it noted pointedly. 'Even the most learned societies in these headstrong times may be a little too previous.'[14]

As for Gibbs, *Chronicle* readers hoping to read the thoughts of the journalist who raised the alarm about Cook were left disappointed. The next day's edition contained nothing at all from him, and as the *Chronicle* continued to report the story the following day, the only time he was mentioned in that edition was as the author of a light-hearted short story it published about the trials of a family getting together at Christmas. Strangely, he seems to have made almost no public comment at all. In fact, in all the reams of newspaper coverage of the verdict, the number of words I have been able to find from Gibbs number just two. Under the headline 'One who is happy', the Danish newspaper *Skive Folkeblad* reported that he had telegraphed his reaction to a Danish friend: 'Simply delighted.'[15]

But while he was not quoted in most newspaper coverage, it was immediately obvious that the disgrace of Frederick Cook was the making of Philip Gibbs. Almost from their first meeting on the *Hans Egede*, Gibbs had staked his credibility on Cook being a liar. And while Gibbs's reporting on Cook had already made him well known, it was only with Cook's seemingly final exposure that Gibbs was established as one of Britain's leading journalists. His elevation to this group was confirmed by perhaps its most famous member, W.T. Stead. After showing so much faith in Cook, Stead graciously wrote to Gibbs to admit that 'I have lost and you have won,'[16] and he was equally magnanimous in public. 'Mr Philip Gibbs of the *Daily Chronicle*, more than any other man, deserves the credit of having discerned from the first the baselessness of Dr Cook's claims,' he wrote in the *Review of Reviews*.[17]

For years to come, Gibbs's fellow journalists would celebrate his intuition in suspecting Cook was lying and the courage and doggedness with which he had pursued him. But Gibbs, at least, realised that whatever journalistic skills he had shown, good fortune had also played an important part from the moment Dagmar Rasmussen had walked into the café on his first evening in Copenhagen. 'It is nearly always luck that is one of the essential elements in journalistic success,' he wrote, 'and sometimes, as in a game of cards, it deals a surprisingly fine hand. The skill is in making the best use of this chance and keeping one's nerve in a game of high stakes ... Truly it [the Cook story] was a queer, exciting incident in my journalistic life, and looking back upon it, I marvel at my luck.'[18]

14

SETTING MATTERS RIGHT

Few people in history have seen such dramatic changes to their reputation in so short a time as those experienced by Frederick Cook in the last four months of 1909. He had started September as a little-known explorer before suddenly becoming one of the world's great heroes, and yet before the year was over he found himself reviled as the perpetrator of one of its biggest hoaxes. The University of Copenhagen's damning verdict was greeted with glee by his enemies, and by his friends and defenders with the stunned and bitter realisation that the man they had placed their faith in seemed to have been lying after all.

With the university verdict coming days before Christmas, New York shops slashed the price of Cook-themed toys, while in Britain pantomimes included topical references to the controversy.[1] An American millionaire renowned for his lavish parties spent a reported £2,000 on a North Pole-themed Christmas dinner at the Savoy in London; the floor of its Winter Garden was covered with plaster snow and its walls and pillars with white chrysanthemums, with models of Cook, Peary, and polar bears completing the scene.[2] In New York, the phrase 'Tell it to the Danes' briefly entered the popular vernacular as a response to a questionable statement.[3]

With the world's newspapers, explorers, and scientists all having given their reaction to the news, the only significant voice that remained silent was Cook's. No one seemed to know where he was, and over the

next few months he became a kind of will-o'-the-wisp figure as newspapers tried and failed to track him down, with unconfirmed sightings
in Marseilles, Naples, Genoa, and Heidelberg in Germany. Every
reported sighting was accompanied by uncertainty about whether it had
really been him, and a German staying in South America came forward
to complain that he was constantly being mistaken for Cook despite not
looking anything like him. The only apparently confirmed sighting was
in Santiago, Chile, in February 1910, when a *New York Times* journalist approached him to ask for an interview and Cook replied that he
wanted to be left in peace.[4]

Newspapers would occasionally make predictions about his imminent reappearance, reporting that he was about to board a boat at Rio
de Janeiro or was expected to arrive in New York to settle down to a
quiet life. But none of these predictions came true, and so the sightings and rumours kept coming. Two Americans had met him on a boat
in Uruguay. He had checked into a hotel in Munich under the name
of Coleman. He was staying in the Colorado mountains. He had been
seen in Etah in Greenland, looking for the records he had left behind
the previous year. As the months passed, the sightings continued, each
one saying more about the way the story continued to grip the public
imagination than about Cook's actual whereabouts. And with Cook
having gone to ground, there was no one to respond to the stream of
denunciations and fresh allegations that followed the University of
Copenhagen's judgement. Just days after the university's verdict, the
Explorers' Club announced it had cancelled his membership because it
now believed his claim to have climbed McKinley was false. Two weeks
later, Cook was expelled by the Arctic Club of America, which he had
himself been involved in setting up.[5]

In May 1910, *The New York Times*, now referring to him as 'one of
the boldest fakers the world has ever known', reported that during the
Belgica expedition a missionary in Tierra del Fuego had lent him a dic-
tionary and grammar book of the Yahgan people that represented his
life's work, and Cook had then failed to return it and passed it off as his
own work.[6] Cook would later describe this as 'one of the meanest and

pettiest charges concocted for Mr Peary', insisting he had given the missionary full credit.

Then, in September 1910, after no word for nine months, Walter Lonsdale received a message from Cook, asking him to arrange an interview with the *New York World* newspaper and giving the address of a dingy room in London's West End where the journalist was to meet him. On the given date, the journalist was waiting in the room and Cook walked in, offering his hand and telling him 'you are the first person to whom I have admitted my identity or to whom I have spoken in my own name, except my wife and children, since I left New York'. They took a cab to an apartment at a hotel in London's theatre district, where Cook chain-smoked cigarettes as he told his story.

'A year's absence from one's country under these circumstances is a long, long time,' Cook said. 'But it was necessary. I was like a deer that had been driven into the cold stream. I simply had to get away from perturbing conditions.' He went on to explain that he had left Europe at the end of 1909 and spent time in Uruguay, Argentina, Chile, and Paraguay, before sailing back to Europe, where he had based himself in London but also visited France, the Netherlands, Switzerland, Italy, the Austrian Tyrol, and Germany. Despite having done nothing more to disguise himself than grow a beard, he had not been recognised in London, he said, even when he had been in the audience at the Royal Albert Hall for a lecture by Robert Peary. Cook assured the journalist he really had reached the North Pole and, while he was not yet recovered from what he called 'those three terrible months of 1909', he was soon expecting to receive evidence that would finally prove his claim. 'I have a full answer to everything, and I will deliver it in my own time,' he said.

The *New York World*'s article about the interview caused a renewed flurry of interest, but journalists who tried to track Cook down could once again find no trace of him. This meant he did not defend himself when Herschel Parker returned from another failed Mount McKinley expedition to announce he had proved Cook's fraud beyond doubt by taking a photograph of a much lower peak that was an almost exact replica of the photograph Cook had claimed was of the summit.[7] Around the same time, Cook's former supporter Knud Rasmussen came forward to say that Etukishook and Ahwelsh, the Inuit who had accompanied Cook north, had now given him their account of the expedition. They had apparently contradicted Cook's account, claimed he had drawn his map to the Pole from his imagination, and accused him of failing to pay them money he had promised them.[8]

Then, on 1 December 1910, *Hampton's Magazine* announced it had found Cook in London and that he had written an article for it. In a press release that was reported around the world, it revealed that Cook had confessed to now being unsure if he really had reached the Pole.[9] The article was published two weeks later, with the words 'Dr Cook's confession' splashed across the front page. The article made clear his 'confession' was that he was not completely certain he had reached the Pole, but this was lost on the many people who reasonably assumed he was confessing to having lied about it. It would later emerge that the magazine proofs Cook had signed off had not contained the passage about his confession, but that it had been inserted into the final article by editors who had paid him handsomely and so wanted it to be as sensational as possible. 'Imagine my heart-aching dismay when ... I found the magazine which was running the articles in which I hoped to explain myself, had emblazoned the sensation-provoking lie over its cover – "Dr Cook's Confession",' Cook later wrote. 'I had made no confession. I had made the admission that I was uncertain as to having reached the exact mathematical Pole ... I felt impotent, crushed. In my very effort to explain myself I was being irretrievably hurt.'[10]

Just after the magazine came out, on 22 December 1910, Cook was a passenger on board a boat arriving in New Jersey and a group of journalists was waiting to meet him. Cook strode towards them, smiling broadly as he handed them a prepared statement that he told them covered everything he wanted to say. 'Any interview I might give would necessarily be fragmentary, and doubtless misleading also, so I shall not now give out any interviews, and any purporting to come from me will not be authorised,' he said. The statement explained that he had returned to the United States to write his *Hampton's Magazine* article and then had gone back to Europe at the end of November. 'I do not know what my plans for the future will be,' it went on. 'I have no plans whatever for going on the lecture platform. I have not returned to America with the intention of making money out of my Arctic experiences. Money did not prompt the writing of my story, as I have seen suggested in certain newspapers. As I have said, I have come back solely for the purpose of rehabilitating myself and my family by setting matters right with my countrymen.'

The journalists were never going to be satisfied with a written statement, and they started firing questions at him. He replied to most of them by saying they would be answered by his forthcoming articles, but he did answer some.

'Well did you climb to the top of Mount McKinley, or is there room for doubt on that score as on the North Pole discovery?' one of the journalists asked.

'No room for doubt this time. I got to the top of that mountain, all right.'

Another asked if he believed Peary had reached the North Pole, and Cook said that while he had always been prepared to take Peary at his word, it would be impossible for Peary to be certain he had reached it, just as he himself was not absolutely sure he had done so.

He was asked if he had any more expeditions planned.

'I am through with exploration. I have had enough. I am here to settle down as an American citizen.' He added that his wife and children had stayed in Europe because his children were at school there, but that he had wanted to come back to face his countrymen and prove he was not a faker.[11]

Back at the Waldorf Astoria and realising that 'my error in so long remaining silent' had allowed allegations against him to go unanswered, Cook once again began to make the case that he really had reached the North Pole. Days after arriving in New York, he angrily rebutted Rasmussen's report about the Inuit by suggesting Rasmussen might be motivated by a grudge because Cook and his companion had not invited

Rasmussen to eat with them in the Arctic because he had smelled. It was a graceless response, and made little sense given that Rasmussen had previously supported him. Cook also argued that Rasmussen had changed his mind on the merits of both his claim and Peary's, which showed he was unreliable. 'The only rational explanation for Rasmussen's irrational course is to credit him with an ambition to get into the limelight,' Cook wrote. 'I hope the outcome has given him the publicity which he has aimed for. But need an explorer stoop to the depths of a literary muck-raker to get public attention?'[12]

A few weeks later, Cook gave a lecture at Hammerstein's Manhattan Opera House, on a stage more used to hosting vaudeville than scientific exposition. He told the audience he had no money to hire a hall, and so was appearing without payment because it gave him the chance to make his case directly to the public. His lecture was regularly interrupted by the mingled sound of hisses and cheers, and when the hisses grew especially loud he defiantly told the audience that 'our children's children will give me a fair verdict'.[13]

In August 1911, he published a memoir of his polar expedition, *My Attainment of the Pole*, in which he reaffirmed his belief that he had reached the Pole. 'When I returned to civilisation and reported that the boreal centre had been attained,' he wrote, 'I believed that I had reached the spot towards which valiant men had strained for more than 300 years. I still believe I reached the boreal centre as far as it is possible for any human being to ascertain it. If I was mistaken in approximately placing my feet upon the pin-point about which the controversy has raged, I maintain that it is the inevitable mistake any man must make. To touch that spot would be an accident. That any other man has more accurately determined the Pole, I do deny.'

My Attainment of the Pole also made it clear that while Cook may have seemed confident and self-possessed during the last few months of 1909, he had in fact been teetering on the brink of mental collapse long before the *Daily Telegraph & Courier* correspondent had noticed signs of strain in the days before he disappeared. In it, he recalled being 'utterly bewildered' by his welcome in Copenhagen, with his main memory of the banquet in his honour being 'the feeling that I must get away without offending these people'. Throughout his time in Copenhagen, he wrote, he 'felt the atmosphere of excitement about me for days, pressing me, crushing me,' while in New York, 'every vestige of pleasure in the thought of the thing I had accomplished left me'. 'I doubt if any man ever lived in the belief of an accomplishment and got so little pleasure, and so much bitterness from it,' he wrote. 'My life was a kaleidoscopic whirl of excitement, for which I found no reason ... There was not a minute of relief, not a minute to think. Coming after two years spent in the Arctic, at a time when nature was paying the debt of long starvation and hardship, the stress of events inevitably developed a mental strain bordering on madness ... I felt alone, a victim of such pressure as, I believe, has seldom been the fate of any human being ... Despair overcame me ... I no longer slept; indigestion seized me as its victim. A mental depression brought desperate premonitions ... I was passing from periods of mental depression to dangerous periods of nervous tension ... As I view myself from the angle of the present, I marvel that a man so distraught did not do desperate things.'

Some of his enemies thought this description of mental turmoil was a lie calculated to explain the poor decisions he had made in late 1909. But it feels genuine. And even if Cook was lying about the Pole, it would be surprising if months of scrutiny and attacks on his character had not taken an emotional toll.

Cook may have hoped *My Attainment of the Pole* would lead to a new appraisal of his polar claim, but it sold poorly and received generally negative reviews; one newspaper sardonically noted it was unsure whether to list it in the fiction or non-fiction section. But it gave him a reason to go back on the lecture circuit, and he booked lectures at venues in South Dakota, Nebraska, Iowa, Kansas, and Missouri. His lecture in Topeka in Kansas stands as an example of the argument he made in lecture hall after lecture hall. 'Public sentiment is changing in my favour,' he told the audience. 'That is because the people are not only fair, but they are intelligent as well. After a sober second thought they realised that there was something crooked about Lieutenant

Peary's charge that I faked the North Pole story, when Peary's story corroborated mine in every important detail. Real scientists now are checking up my account with Peary's account, and checking both with known data of the polar country. The further the investigation goes, the better it shows up for me. In a little while the people will have all the facts, and then they will say there is no doubt that I discovered the North Pole.'[14]

After a series of lectures in America, Cook decided to return to Europe to continue making his case there. On 10 October 1911, he and his wife and children boarded a liner to take them across the Atlantic, arriving just minutes before it finished boarding to find a group of reporters waiting.

'All explorers are judged by their final data, and I feel that it is in this manner I should be judged,' Cook told them. 'So was Peary judged, and so should I be judged. I am going to Europe to present scientific data to various institutions to prove that I was as near the Pole as any man ever got.'

'Will Copenhagen be in your itinerary?' one of the reporters shouted after him as he walked towards the ship. He turned and smiled at them, and then went aboard without answering.[15]

If the reporter's question was a guess, it was a good one. In 1909, Copenhagen had welcomed Cook as a hero, and his last memory of the city was of looking back at thousands of people cheering him. In the two years since, he had been abandoned by many of his supporters, criticised by newspapers around the world, and faced multiple allegations of dishonesty. It made sense that he would want to return to a place where he had experienced almost universal acclaim.

But the Copenhagen of October 1911 was very different from the Copenhagen of September 1909. The University of Copenhagen's report had turned the Danish public against its former hero, with the belief that they had been humiliated before the world transforming their adulation into anger.

In the Copenhagen of October 1911, crowds still gathered to see Cook as he arrived at the station, but this time they came not to cheer but to boo. He was there to give a lecture to an audience of 1,500 people in the same hall where two years previously he had addressed the Royal Danish Geographical Society in the presence of King Frederick and Crown Prince Christian. Then, the audience had hung on his every word and he had to pause to wait for the rapturous rounds of applause to subside. This time, he was openly jeered, his lecture interrupted by angry arguments between those supporting him and those who were there to protest his appearance.

If there was one thing about Cook everyone agreed on, it was that he was extraordinarily cool under pressure, and he ignored the boos and jeers and carried on with the lecture. But then a large man stood up, and the audience turned to see that it was Carl Martin Norman Hansen, the poet and explorer who had previously been so staunch in his support of Cook that he had apparently been prepared to fight Philip Gibbs to defend his honour. Now, he spoke out to condemn him. To wild cheers from some and shouts to be quiet from others, Norman Hansen condemned Cook as the world's greatest scoundrel who, having betrayed the trust of the Danish people, should be expelled from Copenhagen. Norman Hansen then walked out, stopping on his way to yell 'Down with Cook!' three times. With Norman Hansen gone, Cook pressed on with his lecture, but when he reached the point where he displayed a photograph of what he said was the North Pole, the booing became so loud that he felt unable to continue. He hurried out of the building, and on the short journey to the Hotel Phoenix was reportedly pelted with rotten eggs and apples and jostled so vigorously that his hat was knocked off. Back at the hotel, the crowd outside was so hostile that a police guard was placed at the entrance.

By any measure, the two years since Cook's return to civilisation had been extraordinary and sometimes humiliating ones. But there can have been few moments since his arrival in Copenhagen in September 1909 quite as desolate as those in his room at the Hotel Phoenix in October 1911. As he heard the boos of the crowd outside and thought back to the jeering faces of his Danish audience and the anger with which Norman Hansen had denounced him, he must have felt a sense of isolation greater than any he had felt during his time in the frozen north, as he realised there was now not a single significant constituency anywhere in the world that still believed in him.[16]

15

TIDES OF HUMAN MISERY

The last few months of 1909 were difficult ones for Philip Gibbs. Not only did he spend them waiting to see if the gambler's courage he had showed in trusting his instinct about Cook would make or break his career, but the publication of his novel did not go to plan.

During his time in Copenhagen, Gibbs had endured the constant worry that one of his articles might provoke an expensive libel suit, but the actual source of his legal problems was something it had not even occurred to him might be contentious. Some of the characters in *Street of Adventure* were based on real journalists he had worked with at the *Tribune*, and he assumed they would be flattered to be included. But shortly after the novel was published in September 1909, he heard dark rumours that seven journalists were so angry about their portrayals that they were considering suing him. 'I had the innocent idea that all my characters, easily identifiable … would like their portraits,' Gibbs wrote. 'But nobody likes their portrait on canvas or between covers unless it is grossly flattering.' Gibbs suddenly felt he 'saw ruin staring me in the face'.[1]

Most of the journalists decided not to go through with their threat, but Randal Charlton, the journalist who had stood with Gibbs as they watched the *Tribune*'s light go out for the final time, issued a libel writ. Charlton's lawyer claimed *Street of Adventure* had jeopardised his client's career by portraying him as a disreputable and worthless character and by holding him up to ridicule and contempt. Gibbs could not believe he was being sued by someone he considered a friend, and found it particularly galling because he had sent Charlton the proofs of the novel before it had been published, offering to change anything he might object to. But not everyone agreed that Gibbs was the wronged party, with one newspaper responding to news of the libel suit by commenting that 'we are not surprised ... [because] the portrait is anything but flattering'.

Not only did the libel action threaten Gibbs with financial ruin, but the publisher responded by withdrawing *Street of Adventure* from circulation just as it was attracting positive reviews.

Then, shortly before the scheduled court case, Gibbs and Charlton bumped into each other in Fleet Street and, after exchanging awkward greetings, Gibbs thought the gentlemanly thing to do was to offer to buy Charlton lunch. They ate at Ye Olde Cock Tavern in Fleet Street, cordially arguing the merits of the case over their meal. But when Gibbs later mentioned the lunch to his lawyers they were appalled, telling him the court would see them dining together so soon before the case as showing such disrespect for its proceedings that it almost amounted to contempt. Gibbs went to see Charlton to tell him what his lawyers had said and Charlton, realising his error in accepting Gibbs's offer of lunch, signed a statement agreeing to withdraw his libel action. So Gibbs was spared the ordeal of the court case, but by then he had already racked up a large legal bill.

Charlton's libel suit did not spell the end for *Street of Adventure*. It was reissued and went on to become one of the most successful novels ever published about Fleet Street, helping inspire generations of young men and women to try a career in journalism and later being made into a film. 'It must seem archaic to the younger generation when they read my characters going about in hansom cabs,' Gibbs later wrote. 'But somehow it appeals because of a youthful spirit in it, and its story of a newspaper life behind the scenes. It was meant as a dread warning to journalistic aspirants, but I am told that it has lured great numbers of young men to Fleet Street where afterwards, no doubt, they have cursed my name.'[2]

But for all *Street of Adventure*'s success, it would be years before Gibbs earned enough from the royalties to pay off his legal fees.

The end of the libel action at least ended Gibbs's legal problems, and around the same time came the news that the University of Copenhagen's verdict had vindicated his decision to accuse Cook of lying. The story of how he fearlessly set himself against the scientific establishment and was proved right fitted so well with journalism's idea of itself at its best that it was repeated in pubs and newsrooms until it became a part of Fleet Street legend. Over a decade later, the *Daily Express* called Gibbs's reporting on Cook 'a triumph of intuition and perseverance'[3] and Frederic Wile, who had covered the story for the *Daily Mail*, wrote in his autobiography that Gibbs has been a 'brilliant young British journalist … [who] certainly was out in front with his bold forecast that Dr Cook's tale would not stand the pitiless light of scientific scrutiny'.[4] A history of British journalism published 30 years after the events in Copenhagen would look back on Gibbs's 'wonderful scoop' and remember how 'Fleet Street felt he had shown great courage in cabling his conclusions as well as astuteness in forming them so quickly'.[5]

His professional rise may not have been as dramatic as Frederick Cook's, but it was remarkable, nonetheless. His success meant the *Daily Chronicle* now regularly trusted him to cover the biggest stories, and so set him on a trajectory for a career that would involve witnessing more history-shaping events than almost any journalist before him.

He was there for the Siege of Sidney Street, when Home Secretary Winston Churchill was ridiculed for the boyish enthusiasm with which he involved himself in a police operation against Latvian revolutionaries who were trapped in a house. Gibbs took cover as 'bullets were flicking off the wall like peas, plugging holes into the dirty yellow brick, and ricocheting fantastically', and he was part of a group of journalists who paid a pub landlord to let them go onto his roof to get a better view. From his vantage point, he watched Churchill directing the operation with 'one hand in his breast pocket, like Napoleon on the field of battle', and he saw the flames start to come from the revolutionaries' house and watched as the roof fell in on them, killing everyone inside.[6]

He reported on the trial of Dr Crippen, one of the twentieth century's most notorious murderers, who killed his wife and was then arrested on board a ship as he attempted to flee to America. Then, after the trial, Gibbs spent several days with Ethel le Neve, Crippen's lover who had fled with him disguised as a boy, who the *Chronicle* paid for her exclusive story. 'In a little restaurant in Soho I sat with Ethel le Neve, day after day, while all the journalists of England were searching for her,' Gibbs wrote. 'Many times she was so gay that it was impossible to believe that she had escaped the hangman's rope by no great distance, and that her lover was a little blear-eyed man lying under sentence of death. Yet that gaiety of hers was not affected or forced. It bubbled out of her because of a quick and childish sense of humour, which had not been killed by the frightful thing that overshadowed her. When that shadow fell upon her spirit again, she used to weep, but never for long … I am certain, as the police were, that she was guiltless of all knowledge and participation in the murder of Mrs Crippen, but she seemed as careless of that crime as any woman of the Borgias when a rival was removed from her path of love.'[7]

Gibbs was one of the first people to learn of the death of Edward VII; he was waiting for news outside Buckingham Palace when he saw the Prince of Wales and his wife leaving in tears, and so he went inside to ask about the health of the king. He was told the king had just died. It meant he was able to phone the news through an hour before it was posted outside the palace. Then, having already been first with news of his death, he was one of a small group allowed to see Edward on his deathbed the next day, where Gibbs thought he seemed 'more handsome than I thought in life'.[8] The following year, he was at Westminster Abbey for the coronation of George V, an honour that meant having to be in his seat a full seven and a half hours before the ceremony. The sandwiches he had with him disappeared, which meant he was weak with hunger as he wrote a long article about the ceremony for the next day's newspaper. He suspected the novelist Marie Corelli, who was sitting next to him, of stealing them, a suspicion that seems plausible given that Corelli was later convicted of food hoarding during the First World War.

Gibbs witnessed the death of Rolls-Royce co-founder Charles Rolls, the first Briton killed in a plane crash, at an air show in Bournemouth in 1910. He also spent time in Paris, watching socialist leader Jean Jaurès address a crowd of 2,000 railway workers ('the heat was frightful and I nearly fainted') and interviewing French Prime Minister Aristide Briand ('handsome, well-groomed, dreamy-eyed') about the unrest there.[9] He visited Ireland shortly before the formation of the Ulster Volunteers militia that further increased tensions between nationalists and unionists. In Belfast, he saw hundreds of cases of rifles in the cellars of the Royal Avenue Hotel and worried Ireland might be on the brink of civil war. Instead of publishing his report, the *Daily Chronicle*'s editor sent it to Winston Churchill as a warning, but Churchill returned the report with a note saying that 'Gibbs has had his leg pulled'.[10]

Gibbs also visited prisons in Portugal to see the conditions royalist prisoners were being kept in following the revolution, visiting 'cells in which poor wretches lay like beasts', kept in chains in almost complete darkness. His articles about the prisons caused an outcry, and shortly afterwards the Portuguese Government declared an amnesty for political prisoners. Whether or not his articles were part of the reason, for months afterwards Gibbs was visited by Portuguese people who wanted to kiss his hand to thank him for helping free their friends and relatives.[11]

His experience of reporting on polar exploration led to him getting to know Ernest Shackleton. Shackleton was a friend of the *Daily Chronicle*'s news editor Ernest Perris, and the *Chronicle* would get the exclusive rights to the story of Shackleton's legendary *Endurance* expedition. When Shackleton stopped at the office to see Perris, Gibbs would join them and listen to Shackleton tell stories of his adventures that Gibbs found so interesting he later regretted not having written them down. Gibbs also kept in touch with Carl Martin Norman Hansen, who sent him letters from his visits to the north, their enmity of 1909 long forgotten, and with Peter Freuchen, who at least once came to stay with Gibbs at his home in Surrey.

At the age of 35, Gibbs had his first taste of war reporting when he was sent to cover the Balkan Wars in 1912. He was briefly arrested on suspicion of spying within hours of arriving in Belgrade, and then had the frustrating experience of trying and mostly failing to get close to the fighting. This gave him what he called 'a secret and rather wicked suspicion that the war correspondent of the old type did not see so much as his imaginative dispatches and thrilling sketches suggested to the public'.[12]

Gibbs may have seen little fighting, but his time in the Balkans gave him enough material for a book about it, and he was also asked by the *Daily Chronicle* to write what proved a successful short book about the sinking of the *Titanic* in 1912. In it, he honoured the 'old qualities of nobility' that the passengers had showed in the face of death, and it gave him the chance to pay tribute to W.T. Stead, who was among the passengers who died. Stead was on deck when it hit the iceberg and reportedly remarked, 'I guess it's nothing serious' and then went back to his cabin to read; he was later seen giving his lifejacket to a fellow passenger and helping women and children into lifeboats, and then standing alone at the edge of the deck, apparently in prayer. 'Among the English passengers there was no more brilliant personality than Mr W.T. Stead, undoubtedly the greatest journalist of the age,' Gibbs wrote of the man who had helped him in Copenhagen despite disagreeing with him.[13]

Gibbs and Stead had become friends since their time in Copenhagen, and they last saw each other shortly before Stead's death, when Stead, a fervent believer in spiritualism, told Gibbs his medium had warned him war with Germany would come suddenly in the month of August.[14] Gibbs laughed off Stead's warning, but he remembered it. That year, he spent time in Germany and was impressed by the German public's friendly attitude towards Britain, but the following year was visited by a Canadian professor who had spent two years in Germany and was convinced it was preparing for war with Britain.

The professor asked Gibbs to write an article for the *Daily Chronicle* to open the public's eyes to the threat, but the *Chronicle*'s editor was doubtful, instead deciding to send Gibbs back to Germany to judge the situation for himself.

This time, Gibbs was disturbed by what he found. A German newspaper editor angrily told him Britain's foreign policy was preventing Germany's development, and a senior clergyman warned that Britain's continuing attempts to humiliate Germany (presumably a reference to the Agadir Incident, when Britain sided with France over Germany) made war seem inevitable. When he met with a group of students in Leipzig, he asked them if they hated England and was shocked when they answered as one: 'Yes.' But he was at least heartened by the attitude of ordinary Germans he met: businessmen, waiters, and railway porters who could see no reason for a war and were contemptuous towards those trying to provoke one. Gibbs was unsure what to think as he returned to Britain, but hoped the lack of popular support meant war was unlikely.[15] He was further reassured when he attended a banquet for a group of German newspaper editors that was hosted by the British press in London in June 1914, hearing German and British newspapermen give heartfelt speeches affirming the unbreakable ties of friendship between the two nations. When he looked back at the banquet years later, it was with a sense of disbelief that just two months later the two countries would be at war.[16]

By late July 1914, a dispute between Serbia and Austria–Hungary had escalated to the point where Britain was on the verge of being drawn into a European war. As British newspapers prepared to cover what would be the biggest news story in history, many of their leading journalists headed to Europe to be close to the action. Gibbs's success in covering the Cook story in 1909 had already opened the way for him to cover some of the biggest stories of the early 1910s. Now, his success in covering those stories meant it was he who the *Daily Chronicle* sent to France on the eve of war, and he crossed the Channel at night as British Navy searchlights swept his boat and French passengers sang 'La Marseillaise' with almost religious fervour.

He was in Paris for the French mobilisation, where the sight of the kisses and farewells of lovers made 'one's very heart weep' with the knowledge that many of them would be saying goodbye for the last time. On the night of 31 July, he was going to get some food at the Café du Croissant after finishing his work, when his way was blocked by police. He asked what had happened and was told that Jean Jaurès, who had been trying to find a peaceful solution to the crisis, had just been dining there when he had been shot dead by a French nationalist. Gibbs could see the seat where Jaurès had been sitting, and was shocked to see it was one he himself had often sat in.

Germany declared war on France on 3 August, and Britain declared war on Germany the following day. Gibbs spent the first few days of the war waiting frustratedly in Paris, his war reporting limited to collecting official reports from the French Government and sending them back to London. He was waiting for permission to join with the British Army, not knowing that War Secretary Lord Kitchener's loathing of journalists meant his request was never likely to be granted. Eventually, he gave up waiting and, despite not being authorised to do so, he and two other journalists left Paris to try to see the fighting for themselves. So began Gibbs's life as a journalistic fugitive, living under constant fear of arrest by his own side as he tried to report on the war and also helping with the war effort by volunteering with an ambulance service.

It was not long before he saw the brutal reality of war. He was shocked by the sight of thousands of French and Belgian refugees, describing them as 'immense tides of human misery'. He saw British soldiers on their way to battle, laughing and joking and enjoying the attention of French girls, and then a few days later saw more British soldiers, this time with bandaged heads and needing help to walk. 'Their faces, so fresh when I had first seen them on their way, had become grey and muddy and streaked with blood,' he wrote. In Diksmuide in Flanders, he was part of an ambulance crew that searched for survivors, walking past dead bodies to reach the wounded as shells rained down on the town square. He recorded how he felt: 'I did not expect to get out of this place alive. I felt rather numb and cold. I was sure that I was very frightened, but my hand was steady when I lit a cigarette. Here comes death, I thought. We shall all be blown to bits. It's very unpleasant. Death is horrible ... But I mustn't show that I'm afraid.'[17]

But he survived, managing to help the wounded onto the ambulance and then escaping to safety. When his luck did finally run out, it came in the form of capture by the British rather than death from a German shell. After weeks of sending news back to London, he was arrested in Le Havre and brought before a general, who told him he had 'a good mind to have you shot against a white wall'. He was held in a hotel for two weeks without any contact with the outside world, but managed to endear himself to the officers who acted as his jailors by buying them drinks, and he eventually persuaded one of them to send a letter to the *Daily Chronicle* to tell them what had happened. The *Chronicle* took up his case with the Foreign Office, which arranged for him to be freed, and he was sent back to Britain with a warning that he would be shot if he tried to return.

Gibbs's war seemed to be over, but then in April 1915 the British Government finally realised the folly of its ban on reporters and set up a system of allowing accredited reporters to stay with the British Army. Despite his arrest, Gibbs was invited to be one of the initial group of correspondents, and he stayed as an embedded journalist until the end of the war. This meant he spent more time covering the war than probably any other British journalist, and his regular despatches were eagerly read by a public hungry for war news. But while this position brought even greater levels of professional success, it came at a price. He was regularly exposed to extreme danger, and had to learn to harden himself against the fear of it. 'Discipline and self-discipline helped one to wear the right kind of mask, to beat down the little devil of fear threatening to clutch at one, and to go through the necessary amount of self-control,' he wrote. But while he learned to cope with being under fire, he never got used to walking along quiet roads and feeling his palms become moist and his feet grow cold as he worried that the German guns might start firing at any moment.

His job also involved seeing appalling levels of death and destruction, and he would regularly visit scenes of battle littered with dead bodies. While some First World War reporters were able to stay detached from the horrors they saw, Gibbs's natural sensitivity meant this was never likely to be true for him. 'A man of great sympathy is Gibbs,' wrote his fellow war correspondent Basil Clarke, 'a man in whom the soul-wound caused by war, and war's horrors and war's sufferings is ever fresh and raw. Such war as this weighs heavy on a mind like that.'[18]

And weigh heavy, it did. 'I suffered a secret agony from first to last because of the slaughter, and the blinding, and the wounding of so many thousands of our men,' Gibbs wrote.[19] 'The effect of such a vision, year in, year out, can hardly be calculated in psychological effect, unless a man has a mind like a sieve and a soul like a sink.'[20] When he returned to Britain on leave, he realised the hard emotional shell he had developed to protect him against the fear and horror was creating a distance between him and his wife, Agnes. 'I saw a tragic look in her eyes when I came back,' he wrote. 'She found a stranger in me because the War had changed me, she thought, and I was no longer the delicate boy she loved – her shy fawn. I found her a little cold, a little distant, with some invisible barrier between us, though I came back to her with passionate longing, and left her again with tears in my heart.'[21]

Gibbs also became angry at what he saw as the incompetence and career-mindedness of many of the senior officers who sent ordinary soldiers to their deaths. Censorship and his reliance on the army meant he could not vent this anger in his despatches, though after the Battle of Loos in 1915 he was invited to breakfast with David Lloyd George and gave a harsh appraisal of Sir John French's leadership during the battle. Lloyd George looked distressed as he listened, and when Prime Minister Herbert Asquith demanded French's resignation soon afterwards, Gibbs wondered if his comments had been partly responsible. Then two years later, Gibbs was invited to dine with Lloyd George, by then prime minister, and he told him the unvarnished truth of what British soldiers were experiencing at the front and how he thought they were being let down by the generals. Lloyd George seemed visibly affected, and the following day he told a newspaper editor that 'I listened last night to the most impressive and moving description of what the war in the West really means ... the thing is horrible and beyond human nature to bear'.[22]

Life as an embedded war reporter involved both supporting the British war effort and informing his readers about developments and, particularly when things were going badly, there was a tension between these two aims. Questions began to be asked about how reliable the reports by Gibbs and the other journalists who served with him were in giving a true picture of the fighting. Gibbs would later admit censorship had been 'irritating',[23] and this, together with a kind of self-censorship and his need to keep the army on side for access, meant that 'during the course of the battles it was not possible to tell all the truth, to reveal the full measure of slaughter on our side, and we had no right to criticism'.

There was a single day, in particular, that became a lightning rod for criticism of Gibbs and his colleagues, and has come to symbolise what their critics saw as their failure. It was 1 July 1916 – the first day of the Battle of the Somme.

Gibbs was awake early, standing silently with the cavalry opposite the village of Fricourt, some 20 miles north-east of Amiens. The British had spent the previous week bombarding the German defences so fiercely that they believed they would now be powerless to resist an attack. So just before dawn, the British guns began what Gibbs called 'a rolling thunder of shell fire' that was so intense it seemed 'as though nothing could live, not an ant, under that stupendous artillery fire'. Gibbs watched the British attack, and after they had taken Fricourt he arrived in the newly captured trenches. He saw the dead bodies of German soldiers, watched a crowd of German prisoners being escorted away and heard lightly wounded British soldiers shouting and laughing, thinking these were indications that things must be going well.

After seeing as much as he could, he started work on his article, knowing it would be the first news of the battle for thousands of people whose loved ones were fighting in it. 'It is not yet a victory,' Gibbs wrote, 'for victory comes at the end of a battle, and this is only a beginning. But our troops, fighting with very splendid valour, have swept across the enemy's front trenches along a great part of the line of attack, and have captured villages and strongholds which the Germans have long held against us. They are fighting their way forward not easily but doggedly. Many hundreds of the enemy are prisoners in our hands. His dead lie thick in the track of our regiments. And so, after the first day of battle, we may say with thankfulness: All goes well. It is a good day for England and France.'[24]

He finished his article by reassuring his readers that 'as far as can be ascertained our casualties have not been heavy'.[25]

Gibbs's article must have given hope to the families of soldiers who read it in the *Daily Chronicle* two days later. But it quickly became clear he had got it dreadfully wrong. Far from a 'good day', it had been – and remains to this day – the single worst day in the history of the British Army. His impression that 'our casualties have not been heavy' was the opposite of reality: on that first day of the battle, almost 20,000 British were killed and another 38,000 wounded. The bombardment that preceded the attack had not damaged the German defences anything like as much as the British had expected, and so the advancing soldiers were mowed down in their thousands.

Gibbs would later try to explain why his initial reporting had been so wrong: 'There was the illusion of victory on that first day of the Somme battles, on the right of the line by Fricourt, and it was not until a day or two later that certain awful rumours I had heard from wounded men and officers who had attacked on the left up by Gommecourt, Thiepval, and Serre were confirmed by certain knowledge of tragic disaster on that side of the battle-line. It looked like victory. In those days, as war correspondents, we were not so expert in balancing the profit and loss as afterward we became.'

In Gibbs's defence, a single reporter could only ever see the fighting immediately around him, and it would have been impossible to judge the success or failure of such a large attack from this perspective. But he could and should have done a better job of reporting it. And even if his first article can be explained away as having been written in the fog of war, it is more difficult to excuse the article he wrote the next day that claimed 'the battle goes on, with success on our arms', and that 'the spirit of our men is so high that it is certain we shall gain further ground, however great the cost'.[26] And then the following day he reported that 'we are gaining new ground and extending our line slowly but steadily',[27] and the day after that 'the battle is developing, I believe, according to the original plan which anticipated slow and steady fighting from one German position to another'.[28] Even as late as 6 July, a full five days after the slaughter of so many thousands, he was still describing it as 'one of the most splendid achievements of British arms ever written down in history'.[29]

Questions about his reporting of the war would dog Gibbs for the rest of his career. Years later, the sense that he had let his readers down was reinforced when David Lloyd George used his war memoir to accuse Gibbs of 'suppressing every check or repulse, and exaggerating with unbridled extravagance every trifling advance purchased at a terrible cost'. Gibbs angrily defended himself, writing that this 'was grossly untrue ... and it was very unjust of Lloyd George of all men to make this accusation against me'.[30]

Gibbs would continue to defend his war reporting. While other embedded war reporters from the First World War eventually came to regret at least some of what they had written, he remained proud of his work during the war and bristled at criticism of it. 'On the whole we may claim, I think, that our job was worth doing, and not badly done,' he wrote, arguing that his work and that of his colleagues meant 'the English-speaking world was brought close in spiritual touch with their fighting men, and knew the best, if not the worst, of what was happening in the field of war, and the daily record of courage, endurance, achievement, by the young that was being spent with such prodigal unthrifty zeal'. 'I verily believe that without our chronicles the spirit of the nation would not have maintained its greatness of endeavour and sacrifice,' he argued.[31]

But as vigorous as his defence of his war reporting was over many years, there is a section in his autobiography where he writes about how the war affected his relationship with Agnes that gives a glimpse – the only hint I have found – of a sense of regret that lay hidden behind the defiance. A regret that was mostly hidden, perhaps, even from himself.

'She [Agnes] hated the despatches of war correspondents always holding out a hope which was never fulfilled, always describing the heroic valour of boys who, of course, were sentenced to death,' he wrote. 'In the end she hated mine, for the same reasons, and I didn't blame her, because that was the truth.'[32]

16

THE PSYCHOLOGICAL ENIGMA

After the humiliation of his lecture in Copenhagen, Frederick Cook abandoned plans for more European lectures and arrived back in the United States on 13 November 1911.

'I was not egged in Copenhagen but was well received,' he told the journalists who met him as he came off his boat. 'It's true there were some slight hostile demonstrations at my lecture in that city, but I had an audience of 2,000 inside the hall, and there were fully 5,000 outside, clamouring for admission.'[1]

Not discouraged by his experience in Denmark, Cook went back onto the domestic lecture circuit. His lecture fees were by now a fraction of what he had earned two years previously, but they were still more than enough to fund a comfortable lifestyle. His lectures were also a chance to win more people over to his side; many of those who heard him speak left convinced he really was the discoverer of the North Pole and had been the victim of a great injustice.

Four months after his return from Copenhagen came the sensational news that Roald Amundsen had reached the South Pole, beating his British rival Robert Falcon Scott by 34 days. Ironically, it was Philip Gibbs's *Daily Chronicle* that secured the exclusive rights to Amundsen's story. The news must have been bittersweet for Cook, the pleasure in his friend's accomplishment tinged with regret at how the exalted status Amundsen now enjoyed had once been his but now seemed lost to him forever.

But Cook could at least take a quiet satisfaction in the small role
he had played in Amundsen's conquest of the South Pole. When
Amundsen had visited him in his hotel suite in Copenhagen in 1909,
he had been planning his own trip to the North Pole. But Cook suggested he try instead for the South Pole because the fact that he and
Peary had now reached the North Pole meant it no longer had the same
lustre. Amundsen worried that Scott had already started planning his
expedition and so would have a head start on him, but Cook reassured
him that Scott was not planning to make proper use of dogs, and so this
could give Amundsen a crucial advantage over him. As he left the room,
Amundsen took a piece of paper from Cook's personal stationery and
used it to write to northern Greenland's chief administrator, asking for
50 sled dogs.[2]

And the very imagery of Amundsen's historic success contained a nod
to Cook's influence – the distinctive wind-deflecting tent Amundsen
erected at the South Pole was identical to one Cook had designed when
they had been together on the *Belgica*. There were also other, less vis-
ible, details of the South Pole expedition for which Cook could claim
credit. Amundsen's sledging strategy was similar to one Cook had suggested, and the design of Amundsen's snow goggles were based on an
idea by Cook.[3] More prosaically, the controversy around Cook's North
Pole claim had taught Amundsen the importance of documenting his
achievement so comprehensively that there could never be any room
for doubt.

Amundsen published a memoir of his South Pole expedition the
following year, and in it he paid warm tribute to Cook, writing that
he had been 'beloved and respected by all' on the *Belgica*, and that 'his
calm and convincing presence had an excellent effect' and 'he mastered
the situation in a wonderful way'. He recalled how Cook had spent his
days caring for the sick and then ignoring his own tiredness to go out to
hunt seals and penguins to provide the fresh meat they needed to treat
the men's scurvy. He also gave Cook most of the credit for the *Belgica*'s
escape from the ice. 'Cook was incontestably the leading spirit in this
work, and gained such honour among the members of the expedition

that I think it just to mention it,' Amundsen wrote. 'Upright, honourable, capable and conscientious in the extreme – such is the memory we retain of Frederick A Cook from those days. Little did his comrades suspect that a few years later he would be regarded as one of the greatest humbugs the world had ever seen. This is the psychological enigma well worth studying to those who care to do so.'

For a public that had long dismissed Cook as a fraud whose credentials were now worth less than nothing, there was an incongruity in him being eulogised as a hero by one of the greatest explorers of all time. This was the enigma of Cook, and it was this enigma that continued to draw audiences to his lectures, first in the United States and then back in Europe for lectures in Germany, Austria, Hungary, and Switzerland, and then back in the United States before Cook crossed the Atlantic again for another European tour. Then, in the winter of 1913, he began to appear regularly on the vaudeville stage, where his fellow performers were novelty acts that included acrobats and a pony ballet. Many people saw Cook's decision to join vaudeville as degrading but, just as he had done in 1911, he argued that it allowed him to continue to make his case directly to the public.

His seemingly never-ending lecture tour also helped fund a political campaign for recognition of his polar claim. He hired a lobbyist who arranged for a copy of *My Attainment of the Pole* to be sent to every member of Congress and twice, in 1914 and 1915, he was able to get a member of Congress to introduce a resolution to recognise him formally as the Pole's discoverer. But, as hard as he fought for Congressional validation, Robert Peary's friends in Congress fought just as hard against him, and both resolutions came to nothing. The Peary camp's political lobbying was just one part of its years-long, no-holds-barred public relations campaign against Cook that included hiring private detectives, distributing anti-Cook propaganda in the towns where he lectured, and planting people in his audiences to ask difficult questions. If anything, the rivalry between Cook and Peary grew more vicious over time; Cook was no longer concerned about lowering himself to Peary's level and now when he took to the lecture stage he would often bitterly accuse Peary of rape and murder for the way he had treated the Inuit.

By the beginning of 1915, Cook had spent five long years trying to persuade people he had reached the North Pole. For all the lecture audiences he had won over and the money he had earned, he was no closer to convincing the world at large of the validity of his claim than he had been at the end of 1909. Now approaching his 50th birthday, he decided to take a break from his campaign to try for one last big achievement that would prove he really was the great explorer he claimed to be. He announced he would attempt to become the first person to climb Mount Everest.

The plan was to make history by climbing Everest, and at the same time make two documentary films about the trip that he hoped would be commercially successful. The voyage he took with two companions lasted from June 1915 to January 1916 and gave him the chance to see much more of the world, as they stopped at Hawaii, Japan, Manila, Singapore, Malaya, Burma, Borneo, India, Manchuria, and Russia. But in terms of exploration and filmmaking, the trip was a failure. Travelling during a world war proved more difficult than he expected, and they were arrested in Burma, detained aboard their ship in Malaya, and there would later be an astonishing claim that German agents plotted to murder them while they were in Manila, planning to assume their identities and travel through the countryside fomenting unrest against the British.

They then spent a frustrating five weeks in Calcutta (now Kolkata), waiting for permission to enter Nepal to try to climb Everest, only to be given the shocking news that they were suspected by the British of being German spies who had arranged a secret shipment of 40,000 rifles that they planned to use to start a revolution. Scarcely able to believe what they were being accused of, they were forced to turn back without setting foot in Nepal. They then journeyed to the interior of Borneo to film the Dayak people, but Cook was disappointed to find they lived less wildly than he had hoped, and then on their way home they made a failed attempt to climb Fuji, Japan's highest mountain.

Back in the United States, Cook's film of his adventures in Borneo did not do well. When he tried to return to lecturing, he found that interest in the polar controversy had declined, partly because of his absence and partly because the public focus on the war made it seem too much like a story from another age.

Perhaps realising he was now too old for serious exploration and that his polar claim was reaching the end of its potential to make money, he decided to try something new, improbably re-emerging in Texas in 1919 as an oil man. Within two years, he was running the Petroleum Producers Association (PPA) in Fort Worth and seemed to have been staggeringly successful, bringing in millions of dollars through a strategy of taking over failing oil companies. But newspapers began asking questions about PPA. How had it generated so much money when it had not had any great success in finding oil? And why did it seem to be in financial trouble despite such extraordinary levels of income? The more questions newspapers asked, the less PPA's success seemed to make sense, and public scrutiny only intensified in January 1922 when Cook was arrested after being found in a hotel room with an 'undressed' woman and a bottle of whisky. He was taken to a police station, where one of the police officers reportedly responded to his protestations of innocence by telling him to 'Tell it to the Danes'.[4] He denied having had alcohol with him and accused his wife, Marie, of setting him up. She promptly filed for divorce.

His problems then deepened when he was one of 91 people indicted as part of a crackdown on dubious business practices in the oil industry. Most of them pleaded guilty, but Cook insisted he had done nothing wrong. The case went to trial on 14 October 1923, where the prosecution alleged PPA had been a colossal fraud, making its money by convincing shareholders in failing companies to throw good money after bad by paying a fee to convert their existing shares into shares in PPA. Many of the companies that PPA absorbed had no assets, the prosecution alleged, and the only reason PPA was interested in them was so it could use their lists of shareholders as 'sucker's lists'. The prosecution set out how PPA had run a massive direct mail operation, where people received letters in

Cook's name promising returns so improbable that the letters amounted to fraud; one of them went as far as to claim PPA's prospects were so certain that people should borrow any money they could to buy stock. The prosecution brought forward a series of witnesses. A Civil War widow told the court she had been so persuaded by Cook's letters that she had sold her carpets to buy more stock, and after giving evidence she angrily shook her finger in Cook's face as she left the courtroom. An expert witness who had analysed PPA's accounts explained how its income from oil was negligible, with most of its money having come from selling shares.

Day after day, Cook sat in court as the prosecution set out its case against him, listening with the same quiet dignity with which he had listened to the accusations in Copenhagen and New York 14 years earlier. Surprisingly, Marie sat dutifully next to him, just months after he had publicly accused her of setting him up to be arrested.

In his defence, Cook pointed to the fact that he had invested his own money in PPA as evidence that he had genuinely believed in it, and he claimed not to have read some of the direct mail letters sent in his name. But his defence was widely seen as implausible, and it was no surprise when the jury found him guilty. But what was a surprise was the sentence: a shocking 14 years and 9 months in prison, and a $12,000 fine. In sentencing him, the judge gave more than a hint that Cook's past controversies were a factor in him handing down such a harsh sentence. 'This is one of the times when your peculiar and persuasive hypnotic personality fails you, isn't it?' the judge told him. 'You have at last got to the point where you can't bunco anybody. You have come to a mountain and reached a latitude which are beyond you … This deal of yours, and this conception of yours, and this execution of yours, was so damnably crooked that I know the men who defended you, defended you with their handkerchiefs to their noses … Your effrontery, vanity, and nerve are so monumental, so cold-steel, so impervious, so adamantine to what I have to say that the only satisfaction I get in saying this is that I know I am voicing the feelings of the decent people of Texas … I cannot express the abhorrence I have for such a crook as you are.'

With the judge's harangue ringing in his ears, Cook was taken away to spend the first night of the six and a half years he would spend behind bars. A journalist who saw him on that first night in the county jail reported that his 'face seems more heavily lined than before' and noted 'an aimlessness to his gait' and 'a droop of his shoulders'. But anyone expecting Cook's spirit to be broken by such a long prison sentence had not counted on the resilience he had showed again and again, and he quickly adapted to his new surroundings. He took up embroidery and showed a real talent for it, and then after being transferred to the federal penitentiary in Leavenworth, Kansas, in 1925, he became popular with both staff and inmates, working in the prison hospital, editing the prison newspaper, and even forming an unlikely friendship with the notorious Chicago mobster Big Tim Murphy.

Cook also spent his time campaigning for his freedom, claiming he was innocent of any crime and that his sentence was excessive. Presidents Calvin Coolidge and Herbert Hoover rejected petitions from him, and when his case went before the Supreme Court the decision to deny him a route to probation was written by Chief Justice William Taft, who as president had sent his congratulations to Cook for having reached the Pole in 1909. As the years went by and each new hope for freedom was dashed, insult was added to injury by the news that great quantities of oil had been discovered in some of PPA's old fields, which meant land that had been sold for next to nothing when PPA collapsed was now worth tens of millions of dollars.

Cook mostly refused to have visitors, but he made an exception in 1926 when he was told that Roald Amundsen had come to see him. 'Remembering ... the debt of gratitude I owed to him for his kindness to me in my novitiate as an explorer, and recalling that I owed my life indeed to his resourcefulness in extricating us from the dangers of that expedition,' Amundsen wrote, 'I felt I could do no less than to make the short journey to the prison and call upon my former benefactor in his present misfortune. Whatever Cook may have done, the Cook who did them was not the Dr Cook I knew as a young man, the soul of honour and kindliness, lion-hearted in courage. Some physical misfortune must have overtaken him to change his personality, for which he was not responsible.'[5]

Cook was deeply touched by his old friend's gesture, and after the visit Amundsen was approached by reporters waiting outside. 'To me, he [Cook] was always a genius,' Amundsen reportedly told them. 'When we were young men together in a Belgian Antarctic expedition I said that if any man ever reached the North Pole, Dr Cook would … I have read Dr Cook's story, written months before Peary's, and I have read Peary's. In Peary's story I have not found anything of consequence that Dr Cook had not already covered. I am not only unconvinced that Dr Cook was a faker, but, on the contrary, I am of the opinion that his story of the discovery is just as plausible as was Peary's.' He finished by telling them Cook was 'the finest traveller I ever saw' and that 'I've never been able to duplicate some of his feats'.[6]

The New York Times's report on Amundsen's comments was headlined 'Amundsen in role of Cook's defender', and Amundsen suddenly found that his unguarded comments had unintentionally reopened the North Pole controversy, in doing so causing fury in American exploration circles. He tried to repair the damage by claiming he had been misquoted and had simply said he had not studied the merits of Cook or Peary's claims, and so was not in a position to form an opinion on them.[7] But the National Geographic Society was so angry that it withdrew a lecture invitation, and he ended his visit to the United States early.

In March 1930, Cook finally heard the news that he had been granted parole. The goodbye given to him by inmates and staff showed he still possessed the extraordinary charisma that had won over the Copenhagen public so completely in 1909. He was given the rare privilege of a farewell dinner, and the following day was mobbed by crowds of prisoners wishing him well as he walked across the prison yard towards freedom. The prison newspaper's article about his departure reported that no prisoner 'was ever held in higher esteem by officials and inmates alike'.

Carrying a small suitcase and wearing an ill-fitting suit, the now 65-year-old Cook was met at the prison gate by a group of reporters.

He told them he was innocent of any crime, but that he had found prison to be an 'isle of rest'. One of the journalists asked him about the North Pole, and he replied that he still believed he had got to within 20 miles of it.

Cook had always been a well of creativity and now, having spent years of long hours in the company of his own thoughts, he fizzed with a dizzying array of ideas about what to do next. He had grand schemes for a futuristic retirement village, for the redistribution of the world's animals to provide more meat, and for feeding seaweed to cows to increase iodine levels in the people who ate their meat. But he failed to find backers for any of them. He tried to establish himself as a campaigner for prison reform, but he could not find a publisher for a book about it and after his first lecture on the subject was warned that it had been in breach of his parole conditions. He wrote a book about how he had survived a winter in the Arctic and finished an autobiography he had started in prison, but could not find a publisher for either. He then tried to go back to working as a doctor and was supposedly interested in the job of prison doctor at Alcatraz, but his application for a licence to practise medicine was rejected because his medical education was now considered out of date.

Having tried and failed to reinvent himself, Cook returned to what he knew best – trying to establish his claim to have reached the North Pole. He told the *Chicago Daily News* that after his death an autobiography would be published that would contain new data that 'will establish irrefutably my claim to discovery of the Pole'. Cook threatened to sue Peter Freuchen for $300,000 after Freuchen wrote in his memoir that Cook had fraudulently claimed to have reached the Pole, but the threat came to nothing. But he did sue Encyclopaedia Britannica Inc. for $25,000 after its junior edition stated his North Pole claim had been 'universally rejected'. He lost the case, the court deciding it had simply been stating a fact about public opinion.

Cook wrote to the American Geographical Society in 1936 to ask for it to start an investigation into his claim to give him the chance to get the credit for it before he died, but he was met with a curt response.[8] 'Dr Cook had an opportunity to present his case 28 years ago,' a spokesman said. 'At that time the Society expressed its willingness to investigate his case. Instead, however, he sent his material to Denmark.' The same year, he addressed the nation on CBS radio. 'I am getting old, and what does matter to me, is that I want you to believe that I told the truth,' he said. 'I state emphatically that I, Frederick A. Cook, discovered the North Pole.'

But while a small band of faithful supporters continued to believe, he did not get any closer to wider public recognition. With his eyesight failing and his energy drained by old age and a lifetime of disappointments, the extraordinary drive that had propelled him forward over so many years began to fade. At the end of 1939, when a friend suggested another lawsuit against someone who had called him a liar, Cook wearily dismissed the idea, pointing out that the results of his previous legal actions 'have been worse than nothing'.

Then on 5 May 1940, he suffered a devastating stroke that left him in a coma. With the end of his life seeming near, a friend appealed to President Franklin D. Roosevelt to pardon him for his fraud conviction, and on 16 May word arrived that Roosevelt had granted the pardon. Cook was told the news in his hospital bed and managed to communicate that he understood what he was being told and that he was happy about it. In the following days, his condition improved to the point where he was able to leave hospital, and Marie came to stay to help look after him. But then he fell into another coma in July and died on 5 August 1940. He was 75.

Cook's name had appeared only sporadically in newspapers in the years since his release from prison, and his death gave them one last chance to remember the story that had so enthralled them in the months after he had emerged from the frozen north. In Britain, it was also a chance for newspapers to celebrate the role of one of their own in exposing him; *The Times*, for example, exaggerated the story by claiming that 'journalists from all parts of Europe raced north to interview the man who in a night had become world famous, but one of them, Mr (now Sir) Philip Gibbs, burst the bubble with one cable to the London newspaper he was representing'.[9] His obituary in *The New York Times* also quoted extensively from Gibbs's original article about his interview with Cook on the *Hans Egede*. The obituaries showed that Cook's story continued to fascinate even after three decades, but were also evidence of the completeness of his failure to convince the world. The story they told of Cook was not of an explorer whose fortitude and resourcefulness had earned the admiration of his peers, but of a man who had been, in the words of the *Daily Herald* in London, 'one of the world's greatest hoaxers'.[10]

Newspapers around the world tried to describe the strangeness of the explorer who still seemed as enigmatic in death as he had in life, and to explain to their readers how his story had seemed so historic and important, before vanishing so quickly into irrelevance. But in all the many thousands of words in the dozens of newspaper articles written to mark his death, perhaps Cook's best epitaph was a sub-heading in the *New York Times* obituary: 'World hero for brief time.'

17

THE WOUNDED SOUL

Philip Gibbs was walking on the road to Mons early on 11 November 1918, when an officer approached him and told him the war was to end at 11 a.m. A soldier with him started dancing in celebration in the middle of the road. They were still walking towards Mons at 11 a.m., and he saw civilians carrying flags in celebration and through the mist he heard a bugle playing.

'Could it be possible?' Gibbs wrote. 'No more blood! No more casualties! No more mutilated, blinded, and shell-shocked men. No more sacrifice of boys, too young to die. Peace! How marvellous! How incredible! How miraculous!'

Later that day, he stopped near the front and marvelled at how quiet it now was; as he heard leaves rustling in the wind, he thought it 'seemed as though God gave a benediction to the wounded soul of the world'. That night, he saw young soldiers laughing as they fired flare guns into the darkness and heard singing and laughter coming through open windows. He went to an officers' club, where one of the soldiers made a toast that was followed by over ten minutes of cheering. 'Some of those who cheered had moist eyes, and were not ashamed of that, because of the memories in their hearts of old pals who had gone missing,' Gibbs wrote. 'And in the midst of all this sound of exultation men had sudden silences, thinking back to the things which have passed.'[1]

He sent back his last despatch from the war the following morning, and then he travelled through Belgium and into Cologne in Germany.

He saw scenes of wild jubilation in recently liberated Belgian cities, joining hands with strangers and dancing in the street. And in Cologne he was heartened by the lack of hostility there, visiting beer halls where British soldiers talked happily and clinked glasses with young Germans. But there were also things that disturbed him. He saw a Belgian man kicked to death in the street for being pro-German, and some of the Germans he met in Cologne told him darkly they had only lost the war because they had been betrayed by communists and Jews.

Then Gibbs returned to Britain. While his coverage of Frederick Cook in 1909 had established him as a leading journalist, the four years he had spent sending back daily reports of the fighting had made him one of the most famous British journalists who had ever lived. The possibilities for his career now seemed limitless, and he soon used his new status to pull off a historic exclusive by securing the first ever newspaper interview with a pope, Benedict XV, in 1919; Pope Benedict did not say anything particularly newsworthy, but the interview was reported around the world. Gibbs then got the chance to go on a lecture tour of the United States, and on arriving in New York was astonished to find he was already well known there because *The New York Times* had published his articles during the war. The following year, he and four other embedded war reporters were knighted, and 1921 saw the release of a film adaptation of his novel, *Street of Adventure*. It was the first of eight films he would contribute to.

But all this professional success did not bring happiness. He was haunted by the horrors he had seen, and the memory of the war loomed so large in his mind that he wrote that 'it obliterated all other adventures, impressions, and achievements'. He was left feeling 'old in the knowledge of human courage and endurance and suffering by masses of men, and utterly changed, physically and mentally'.[2] When he looked back years later, the mental state he described would today be recognised as post-traumatic stress disorder: 'I was incapable of being happy at that time, because the war had left me with frayed nerves and a painful obsession. I could not forget the tragedy of the war and the slaughter of youth. I was obsessed with its horror, and felt guilty of having a car, of living in comfort in this good house and lovely garden when so many men who had been the heroes of the war were trudging about the streets looking for jobs.'[3]

He struggled with feelings of anger towards people who had not been at the war, writing that 'as an onlooker of war I hated the people who had not seen, because they could not understand'. When an acquaintance casually asked if he had had an interesting time in France, Gibbs wrote that he had wanted 'to kill [him] because of his smug ignorance, his damnable indifference, his impregnable stupidity of cheerfulness in this world of agony'. And he was surely writing about himself when he made a general point about what it had been like for journalists returning from the war: 'Those young writing-men who had set out in a spirit of adventure went back to Fleet Street with a queer look in their eyes, unable to write the things they had seen, unable to tell them to people who had not seen and could not understand. Because there was no code of words which would convey the picture of that wild agony of peoples, that smashing of all civilized laws, to men and women who still thought of war in terms of heroic pageantry.'[4]

Gibbs also felt bitter towards the political leaders whose decisions had led to the war, and towards the generals whose mistakes he blamed for so many deaths. And he felt growing anxiety about the future, worrying that the Treaty of Versailles was a 'peace of vengeance, and a peace of greed and a peace of hypocrisy',[5] and that 'the Governments of Europe [had] arranged a peace which was to be a preparation for new wars'.[6] It was an anxiety that was deepened by what he saw on his travels. He visited dosshouses in London filled with ex-servicemen, on a trip to Vienna witnessed extreme hunger and visited a hospital filled with children with rickets who he thought 'looked like starved monkeys', and in Hungary he found great anger about the territory they had lost.[7] In Germany, he found a deep-seated hatred of the French that 'made me afraid for the future', and on his lecture tour of the United States he met Yale students who told him they hoped they would soon get their chance to fight in a war, just as their older brothers had done.[8] Conscious he was 'alive after a war which had killed so many', Gibbs saw it as his duty to try to help avert another war, and the cause of peace became almost a personal crusade. 'Such a war must never happen again, we thought, and it was for us to prevent it so that the next generation of youth would be saved from its agonies and sacrifice,' he wrote. 'I dedicated myself to peace, and made a vow in my heart that I would work for it above all other motives and interests.'[9]

In 1920, he published a memoir of the war called *Realities of War*. He had written it, he explained in the preface, out of a belief that 'the world must know and remember, not only as a memorial of men's courage in tragic years, but as a warning of what will happen again – surely – if a heritage of evil and folly is not cut out of the hearts of peoples'. The following year, he published another book called *The Hope of Europe*, in which he urged the world's youth to build a movement for long-term peace and understanding between nations. Following the war, Gibbs was effectively working for David Lloyd George, who had become the first serving prime minister to control a popular newspaper when a group of his friends bought the *Daily Chronicle*. Gibbs's feelings towards Lloyd George were a cocktail of 'admiration strangely mixed with regret, affection twisted by anger and annoyance, amusement causing laughter with a groan in it'. And whatever affection Gibbs felt for Lloyd George, he also felt real hatred towards him for 'helping to arrange a Peace which seemed to me to guarantee the certainty of new and more dreadful war'. He was also disgusted by how British violence in Ireland had 'dishonoured the old fame of England by abandonment of justice, chivalry, and the spirit of liberty for which so much of England's youth had died'. Given Lloyd George was responsible for the British policy in Ireland, Gibbs felt he could no longer in good conscience work for the *Chronicle*, and he decided to resign.[10]

Just as he had been so many times in the first years of the century, Gibbs was again an out-of-work journalist. But this time unemployment did not bring financial worries, but instead gave him the freedom to develop a lucrative and varied freelance career writing articles, novels, and non-fiction books. His non-fiction books were generally political commentaries on Europe that warned about the future, but he also published a memoir in 1923, which included him telling for the first time the story of how he had exposed Frederick Cook. It was, he wrote, 'the only important scoop that I can claim' and 'a great game which I thoroughly enjoyed'.[11] Remembering the moment Cook showed his hands to the audience at the University of Copenhagen, Gibbs admitted to thinking that perhaps Cook really believed he had been to the Pole: 'Sometimes, remembering the manner of the man, I am tempted to think so still – though now there is no doubt that he never went near his goal.'[12] The same year, his achievement in exposing Cook was covered again in British newspapers when they reported on Cook's fraud conviction.

Gibbs's novels after the First World War looked at the same kind of issues as his non-fiction: one was about ex-soldiers adjusting to peacetime, another about the situation in Europe, and another about Anglo-German relations. They sold well, with his novel *Heirs Apparent* the fourth-bestselling novel in the United States in 1924, and by the middle of the 1920s *The Westminster Gazette* thought that 'Sir Philip Gibbs stands, in the minds of most people, for the journalist–novelist par excellence'.[13] But his novels' success owed more to the celebrity of their author than the literary merit of the fiction; in the view of Gibbs's biographer, Martin C. Kerby, they 'became forums for extended political discussions where narrative is clearly secondary to proselytizing', with 'an element of the production line about some of them'.[14] Gibbs once dined with H.G. Wells and was surprised when Wells told him he considered it a good evening's work if he had written 500 words he was happy with. Gibbs's response that he might write 5,000 words in that time perhaps goes some way to explaining why he was a better daily newspaper journalist than he was a novelist.[15]

No longer having a job also meant he could follow the success of his visit to the United States with further lecture tours there in 1920 and 1921.[16] Gibbs's natural shyness meant he had found his first lecture at Carnegie Hall one of the most terrifying experiences of his life; he had been so consumed by nerves that he worried he was going to be sick on stage. But he was warmly applauded and, while he never completely conquered his nerves, they lessened over time. His lectures also gave him the chance to see the United States and meet some of its leading politicians, including President Warren Harding and future President Herbert Hoover. At the end of his 1921 visit, a banquet was held in his honour at the Waldorf Astoria, the same hotel that had hosted the banquet celebrating Cook's return to New York 12 years earlier. As well as being well paid for his lectures, Gibbs was amazed by how much American magazines were willing to pay for short stories, which 'helped to butter my bread and even provide a little jam'.[17] The *Salt Lake Tribune* may have been exaggerating when it called him the 'most popular Englishman that has ever talked to the American public and written for the American Press',[18] but the fact that it printed it gives a sense of how well known he was there in the early 1920s.

As well as using his new-found freedom to make money, he spent time campaigning for the causes he cared about. He became vice president of the Ex-Services Welfare Society, and while in the United States appeared before the House Committee on Naval Affairs, giving his views on British foreign policy, Ireland, and European politics. Later, he sat on a Royal Commission into the armament trade but became disillusioned after its recommendations were ignored.

He continued to travel, seeing with his own eyes how the international situation was developing. He went to Russia on behalf of the Imperial Famine Relief Fund, where he saw levels of hunger and destitution that were in their way as shocking as the things he had seen during the war. He was on a train platform in Petrograd (today St Petersburg) and watched with horror as a train arrived on the platform and its doors opened to reveal that almost all its passengers were dead, victims of typhus. At one hospital, patients had to huddle together for warmth, while at another he was greeted by emaciated nurses who desperately grabbed at him and begged him for food. In Kazan, after Gibbs and his colleagues attended a performance of *Carmen*, the opera company followed them back to their billet and begged them for food.

He visited Essen in Germany after the French invasion of the Ruhr in 1923, talking to German workers who told him they would rather starve than follow orders from the French. He was in Berlin during hyperinflation, seeing American journalists who exchanged their dollars into German marks 'living like princes for next to nothing, drinking too much, shouting too much',[19] and visiting a department store where he saw staff mark up the prices twice in the time it took him to do his shopping. While in Germany, he interviewed two Reichsbank officials who both began to weep as they talked to him. But there were also hopeful moments – in 1926, he cheered from the public gallery in Geneva as Germany was admitted to the League of Nations.

Above all, Gibbs continued to write, and to warn. In 1930, for example, he wrote an article for *The New York Times* to mark the twelfth Armistice Day, using it to express his fears that the fact that 'nations are arming again' and 'old hates are reviving' meant that 'it is still only an armistice'.

His hopes for peace took a dark turn with Hitler's rise to power in Germany in 1933. During a visit to Germany the following year an old waiter in Munich, who Gibbs knew from previous visits, told him in a low voice that the Nazis were taking Germany in a dangerous direction.[20] Gibbs wrote for *The New York Times* that Nazism was 'very dangerous' and contained 'something in it not belonging to European traditions', but he reassured his readers that 'Adolf Hitler says he wants peace, and I believe him'.[21]

With extremism on the rise in Europe, Gibbs worried about the ability of Britain's politicians to meet the challenge of the new age. He got to know Prime Minister Ramsay MacDonald, and was once getting a lift with him in his car when MacDonald turned to him.

'My dear Philip,' he said. 'I am a broken man. I can't put two sentences together, and I can't put two ideas together. I am blind, and old, and useless.'

'He grasped my hand and clung to it like a small boy needing comfort,' Gibbs later remembered, 'and my heart was filled with pity for him, and I was stirred by the poignancy of this tragedy. But when I left him I was disturbed by the thought that a man in this state of mind and body should be Prime Minister at such a time in our history.'

Gibbs spent the 1930s continuing to be obsessed with maintaining peace, at one point writing that 'all I think about is how to avoid another world war'.[22] But as repulsive as he found Nazism, his hatred of the Treaty of Versailles and his desperation to avoid war combined to blind him to the scale of Hitler's threat. 'All that Hitler had done ... was to regain for Germany sovereign rights over her own territory free from foreign control or interference and stand equal with other powers,' Gibbs wrote in 1937 about Germany's breaches of Versailles. 'Have we no imagination, no touch of generosity, no sympathy with a nation that breaks its fetters? I dare to say that Hitler, in these acts, was heroic in his liberation of the German folk from foreign control and inequality of justice.'

And his verdict on Hitler's claims to want peace with Western Europe? 'I am convinced he spoke with sincerity.'[23]

Apart from one occasion when members of the RAF passed him secret documents about the strength of the Luftwaffe that he clandestinely delivered to Winston Churchill, Gibbs's sympathies lay with the appeasers. In fact, after Gibbs enjoyed dining with Churchill and being given a tour of the grounds of his home at Chartwell in Kent, he was left feeling irritated after Churchill accused him of being 'one of the goody-goodies ... one of the pacifists'. Gibbs was certainly not a pacifist, but he thought the Sudetenland crisis was a case of Germans wishing to 'join their own folk'. And when it came to the rest of Czechoslovakia, he could not understand why British soldiers should die defending a 'hodge-podge of races under the domination of the Czechs'.

He continued to believe war could be averted even after interviewing Heinrich Himmler in March 1938. There is an irony that the journalist whose scepticism of Frederick Cook had been the making of his career was unable to see the true nature of the man who would go on to be the architect of the Holocaust. 'He looked like a professor at a university, or even perhaps an artist,' Gibbs wrote. 'There was nothing repulsive about him. On the contrary, he was genial, vivid and humorous. It was difficult to believe I was in the presence of a most damnable villain.'

Himmler jovially introduced himself as 'a man whom your English newspapers call "the worst man in Germany"', and then showed Gibbs a map of the globe and, laughing, pointed to all the countries that fell under the British Empire and asked Gibbs why the British begrudged Germany its *Lebensraum* ('living space'). He then asked why the English thought Hitler was preparing for war.

'Many people in England think that Hitler, after rearming, may be tempted to play the part of Napoleon and attack other people's frontiers,' Gibbs replied.

'That is not only not the truth but the very opposite of the truth,' Himmler laughed. 'I know what is in Hitler's mind, and that is not part of it. After all, we have read a little history. We know something about Mr Napoleon. We know what happened to him. We also know that if Hitler was to attack other people's frontiers and march across Europe, as you suggest, it would be for Germany the road to ruin. That is a way we shall not go.'

Gibbs seems to have been prepared to believe Himmler because he was telling him something he badly wanted to be true. But even looking back on the interview years later, he still struggled to understand: 'Why did he say that? If he were lying to me that would be easy to understand, but surely he would not have lied in such a phrase? He need not have prophesised that a war of aggression would be for Germany the road to ruin. Even now I find its psychology inexplicable.'

When Germany occupied Czechoslovakia in March 1939, Gibbs wrote to *The Times* repeating what Himmler had told him, ending his letter by suggesting that 'Herr Himmler may be right in his prophecy as to what will happen at journey's end'.[24] He later wondered if this was the reason his name was added to a Nazi list of public figures to be arrested in the event of a German invasion.[25]

As late as the summer of 1939, Gibbs was continuing to write that he believed 'war even now is not inevitable'.[26] We can only imagine his feelings as he and Agnes sat listening to the radio in their house in the village of Shamley Green in Surrey on 3 September 1939, as Prime Minister Neville Chamberlain announced the declaration of war.

'So it has come,' Agnes said to him, and they looked sadly into each other's eyes.

Gibbs used an article to mark the first Armistice Day of the Second World War to explain what the war meant to those who had spent the previous two decades trying to avoid it: 'We of the older ranks who have dedicated ourselves to the prevention of another war stand amid the ruin of our hopes and false dreams. We failed. The forces of evil have come out against us, so that this young generation may have to pay the price of blood to save all which we believed had been won and secured by the spirit of the dead who are around us today.'[27]

Agnes had been in poor health for some time. She had struggled to find happiness after the First World War, and she had become so unwell that she needed two life-saving operations. By 1939, she was ill with liver cancer and a month after war was declared, on 4 October 1939, she died. The loss of 'my beautiful and beloved Agnes' was a devastating blow that left Gibbs bereft.

Shortly after her death, the 62-year-old Gibbs travelled to France to resume his previous career as a war reporter for the *Daily Sketch*. For a man who had spent two decades haunted by memories of war, returning to the places he remembered from the First World War was a surreal experience. 'I had the queerest sensation of being a ghost and walking among ghosts,' he wrote. 'For every village into which I went, and every bit of country through which I passed, every town in which I halted with the younger crowd of war correspondents, was haunted by the young officers and men of the old war ... All over this countryside were the war cemeteries with their rows of crosses in crowded ranks. There below the soil lay the lads whom I had known ... who knew their chances were one in four when they went over the top, and less than that the second time. Those graves, those dead, the living spirit of those men who had never been put out of my mind all the years between. It was the massacre of those young men ... [that] made me so passionate for peace, so hard-working for it in all my books and in every line I wrote ... I was ghost-haunted. I myself was a ghost of that previous war ... Everything looked the same. The

Vimy Ridge looked the same, through dank mist or a flurry of snow. The British soldiers in Arras were just like those others – their fathers – with the same cut of the jib ... They were singing the same songs.'[28]

Gibbs spent much of the first nine months of the war in France, though his failing eyesight meant he sometimes had to rely on others to lead him by the hand through the streets and to dictate his copy over the telephone. He visited the Maginot Line and was impressed by it, but worried the French were putting too much faith in it, presciently fearing the Germans might be able to go around it. He was in Paris when the Germans began their attack westwards the following May, deciding to stay there despite a warning from the military 'to go back to England while the going is good'. But each day brought worse news, and Gibbs heard bombs exploding in the distance, saw long lines of refugees on his drives into the countryside, and saw packed trains leaving for the south. With the Germans' arrival in the city seeming imminent, he was ordered to leave and flew back to Britain.

Leaving Paris marked the end of his career as a war reporter, and back in Britain he spent time in London seeing how people were holding up under the nightly bombing, while at his home in Surrey he would look out of his window at night to watch the German bombers like 'black bats of death' as they skimmed the tops of trees on their way to London. He spent much of the rest of the war writing novels and sometimes appearing on the radio and, for all the mental anguish his war reporting had brought him, after D-Day he found himself envying the journalists who were over in Europe. The war also gave him the chance for a last lecture tour of the United States in 1941, during which he met President Franklin D. Roosevelt, who the previous year had granted a pardon to the dying Frederick Cook.

On VE Day, 8 May 1945, Gibbs went out into Shamley Green to join the celebrations. As he watched effigies of Hitler being burned and listened to the sound of children laughing, his mind went back 27 years to the end of the last war, thinking about how it had sown the seeds of the war they had just fought and hoping that this time would be different. 'The end of another war,' he wrote, 'a war which ought never to have been fought, and need never have been fought, if, after the last, there had been a little more wisdom, a little more morality, a little more virtue in us. Was it the end of war itself? If not, then the world is just a lunatic asylum and we are all poor fools.'[29]

In 1946, Gibbs published a second autobiography, *The Pageant of the Years*, and he ended it by worrying that the tension between the United States and the Soviet Union could lead to a third world war. Just as he had done after the First World War, he called for people to join together in a crusade to save civilisation from 'the power politics of evil leaders'.[30] In the years that followed, Gibbs continued his writing, but his voice now seemed less relevant, as both international politics and society had moved on while he continued to look back to the past. In the words of his biographer Martin C. Kerby, 'he retreated to a conservatism steeped in nostalgia as a defence against a world he no longer understood'.[31]

Gibbs continued his prodigious literary output, and by the time of his death he had written a staggering 91 books. But nothing he wrote in his later years approached anything like the success of *Street of Adventure*; *The Times*'s obituary of Gibbs would include the blunt verdict on his novels that 'their survival as literature is undeserved'. Given his success as a novelist had owed so much to his celebrity, as his fame faded in the post-war world, so their sales dwindled. But Gibbs kept writing almost to the very end. He sent his last book to his publisher on 9 March 1962, and then the following day, aged 84, he died of pneumonia.

The quality of the literary work he left behind may not have been high enough to ensure his name would live on, but by any measure, the life he had lived had been extraordinary. His interview with Frederick Cook had started him on a journey that both placed him at the heart of historic events and condemned him to bear witness to scarcely imaginable levels of human suffering. It was a career that was incredibly successful but that became defined by his years of crusading against a coming calamity driven by forces he was powerless to resist. What does such a life teach a person? It was a question Gibbs himself attempted to answer in *The Pageant of the Years*: 'If I have learned anything it is that pity is more intelligent than hatred, that mercy is even better than justice, that if one walks around the world with friendly eyes one makes good friends.'

18

EPILOGUE

Robert Peary died two decades before either Gibbs or Cook, on 20 February 1920, aged 63. While Frederick Cook had a relatively modest funeral, Peary was buried as a national hero with full military honours at Arlington Cemetery, the US vice president and chief justice in attendance. Later, a globe-shaped monument with a bronze star at its northernmost point was erected by his grave, inscribed on one side with words attributed to Hannibal and which had inspired him when trapped in an Arctic storm: 'I shall find a way or make one.' On the other side of the monument was a four-word epitaph that signalled the recognition he had craved his whole adult life: 'discoverer of North Pole'.

It was a fitting end for the conqueror of the North Pole – one last accolade for a hero in whose honour ships had been named, postage stamps issued, and whose legacy was assured by the number of times his name appeared on maps: Peary Land, Peary Glacier, Peary Nunatak, Cape Peary, Peary Bay, Peary Channel, Mount Peary, and even a crater at the Moon's North Pole have all been named after him. When Peary had returned from the north in 1909, his claim to have reached the Pole was not the subject of anything like the controversy that had consumed Cook's claim; after examining Peary's records, the National Geographic Society announced itself satisfied he had reached the Pole. He then spent the following year collecting honours from the societies and universities of Europe, and Congress passed a Bill in his honour that awarded him the rank of rear admiral and a pension of $6,000 a year for life.

But for all the acclaim, questions lingered. Given the greasiness of the food he had eaten on his expedition, why were the pages of his diary so clean? Why did one of his supporters fail in an attempt to find Crocker Land, the huge land mass he said he had discovered in 1906? And why did he perform poorly under questioning during the Congressional hearings? The absence of good answers to these questions meant some people doubted him still. But the world at large believed in him for the simple reason that scientists and explorers knew that Peary was some-one whose word could be trusted. Roald Amundsen summed it up in his memoir: 'I know Admiral Peary reached the North Pole. The reason I know it is that I knew Peary ... The answer to any doubt on that score is simply that Peary was not that kind of man.'[1] Ernest Shackleton agreed, telling journalists that 'Peary is a man of unquestioned integrity, and every word of his may be relied upon'.[2] This meant Peary died in the knowledge that the four-word epitaph on his grave was the last word on the question of the discovery of the North Pole.

But for all the accolades from scientific societies and the unwavering faith of his supporters, the continuing whispers had so greatly ran-kled with the fiercely proud explorer that he spent his last few years reluctant to talk about his achievement. On hearing news of his death, Shackleton said he had no doubt that the end of Peary's life had been embittered by the North Pole controversy.[3] As part of its report on Peary's death, *The New York Times* tracked down Frederick Cook to Santiago in Chile, asking him for his reaction to the news. Just as he had done to the same newspaper when it had found him in the same city ten years earlier, Cook replied that he just wanted to be left in peace.[4] But given how spectacularly and publicly their life stories had collided in 1909, newspapers could not tell the story of the life of the discoverer of the North Pole without also telling the story of the fraud who had tried to steal the glory from him. So Peary's obituaries were filled with regret at how Cook's lies had sullied one of the greatest feats in the history of exploration.

But there is another way of looking at it. Perhaps Cook's claim to have reached the Pole helped Peary rather than harmed him. When suspicions were raised that Cook might have been lying, perhaps this made it seem inconceivable that two liars could come along at the same time. And perhaps the damage the Cook controversy caused to the reputation of polar exploration meant scientists were less eager to rigorously scrutinise Peary's claim.

In the decades following Peary's death, occasional books and articles were published questioning whether he really had reached the Pole, but they never seriously threatened his position as its widely accepted discoverer. For one thing, his records were not publicly available and so there was little evidence for historians to examine. But then in 1983, more than 70 years after the National Geographic Society verified his claim, a film was shown on American television that changed everything.

Starring Rod Steiger as Peary and Richard Chamberlain as Cook, the film told a different story to the one generations of American children had been brought up to venerate – one in which Cook was the hero and both Peary and the National Geographic Society were the villains. The National Geographic Society was furious, with National Geographic publishing an editorial calling the film a 'blatant distortion of the historical record, vilifying an honest hero and exonerating a man whose life was characterized by grand frauds'. The National Geographic Society was so angry that it persuaded Peary's family to lift the restrictions on his papers, thinking this was the only way to prove the film's portrayal of Peary was a calumnious lie.[5] The society then asked the British explorer Wally Herbert, who himself had reached the North Pole in 1969, to assess Peary's papers. Herbert duly did so, but rather than confirming the validity of Peary's claim, he wrote an article setting out his explosive finding that Peary may not have got to within 30 miles of the Pole.

This was hugely embarrassing for the National Geographic Society and so, not liking the conclusion of Herbert's assessment, it commissioned another. This second report came to the more comfortable conclusion that Peary had indeed reached the Pole, but its credibility was undermined by it containing basic errors of fact, and then Herbert published a book called *The Noose of Laurels* that argued that Peary had fallen short of the Pole. The allegations sent shockwaves through the world of exploration, leading *The New York Times* to publish an extraordinary correction in which it admitted it had been wrong to claim, in an article published 79 years previously, that 'one thing certain is that the North Pole has been discovered by an American explorer'. In righting this historic wrong, *The New York Times* now admitted that 'most authorities today agree that no one has an untainted claim to be first – neither Cook, nor Peary'.[6]

Over the next few years, various experts weighed into the debate, some supporting Peary's claim and others dismissing it. But what was now clear beyond any doubt was that Amundsen and Shackleton's belief in Peary's honesty had been misplaced. The more Peary's career was studied, the clearer it became that it had been littered with lies and exaggerations, the most glaring examples being that we are now sure Crocker Land does not exist (and the evidence suggests Peary lied about it rather than made a mistake) and that there are serious doubts about his claim to have broken the 'farthest north' record in 1906. Today, National Geographic describes Peary's polar claim as being 'in dispute', but probably the most reliable verdict comes from the writer Robert M. Bryce, whose fair-minded and exhaustive investigation concluded that, while we cannot be certain he did not reach the Pole, 'there seems to be no evidence that proves Peary reached the North Pole in 1909', but 'there is compelling circumstantial evidence that he did not'.

While the view of Peary's claim has changed dramatically in the years since his death, Cook's reputation has stayed the same. In contrast to his rival, there were no landmarks that bore his name until 1986, when Cook Summit in Antarctica was named in recognition of his contribution to the *Belgica* expedition. Cook does still have his champions, some of whom have written books with titles like *Winner Loses All* and *The Case For Dr Cook*, in which Philip Gibbs emerges not as a journalistic hero but as a young reporter on the make, his articles dismissed as 'diatribes'[7] and an emphasis put on how he was 'taken off the story' when Cook returned to New York.[8] For many years, the Frederick A. Cook Society was the keeper of the flame, continuing to argue that Cook was a victim of his own naivety and a vicious propaganda campaign, and that enough in his descriptions of the North Pole and Mount McKinley has been borne out by subsequent exploration to merit a re-evaluation. On 21 April 2008, dozens of the society's members gathered in New York to commemorate the centenary of the date Cook claimed to have reached the Pole, brought together by their shared belief in an achievement that the world at large had long dismissed as a lie.[9]

It is not the role of this book to judge the merits of Cook's claims. Like Gibbs, I came to this story knowing next to nothing about Arctic exploration and, as much as I have learned through researching this book, I am a still long way from being qualified to give a view. But Robert M. Bryce has spent years assessing the evidence, and his view is that it overwhelmingly shows Cook lied about both climbing Mount McKinley and reaching the North Pole. In both cases, Bryce believes Cook did not set out intending to deceive, but thinks that he decided to fabricate his claims when it became clear he would not be able to achieve his goals. It is hard to reconcile Bryce's conclusion with the apparent sincerity with which Cook showed his hands to the audience at the University of Copenhagen, or the determination with which he tried to prove his claim over so many years. But, for what it's worth, I agree with him.

But if neither Cook nor Peary were first to reach the North Pole, who was? The answer is not straightforward. Naval officer Richard E. Byrd claimed to have flown over it in a monoplane in 1926, but his claim is widely disbelieved. Roald Amundsen definitely did fly over it three days after Byrd's attempt, but does flying over the Pole in an airship really count as having reached it? And, if not, does standing on the spot after flying there count, as a group of Soviets did in 1948? Or what about the submarine that got there in 1958, or the snowmobile in 1968? Or can you only really claim to have reached the Pole if you have made it there the same way Peary and Cook tried to, without support or motorisation? If so, it was not until 1986, three-quarters of a century after Peary and Cook's expeditions, that Will Steger led the first verified expedition to the North Pole by dog sled without resupply. So, while the story of the quest for the South Pole had a neat ending with Amundsen beating Scott to it in 1911, the question of who was first to reach the North Pole has no definitive answer because it depends on what you think reaching it even means.

And while the question Gibbs posed in the article he wrote on Cook's first day in Copenhagen – had he really reached the Pole? – has long been answered to most experts' satisfaction, another question remains. How could an explorer who showed such remarkable compassion, resilience, and creativity during the *Belgica* expedition be the same man who a decade later attempted perhaps the most cynical fraud in the history of exploration? When Amundsen came to reluctantly accept that Cook was lying about the Pole, he concluded it was so out of character with the Cook he had known that 'some physical misfortune must have overtaken him to change his personality'. But while the idea of Cook as a good man who somehow became a bad man fits with the way we categorise people, it is too easy.

Even before the *Belgica*, Cook was prepared to lie when it suited him. He lied to journalists by telling them he had not received any complaints about the disastrous tourist trip he led to the Arctic, and he later lied about the story of how he had joined the *Belgica*, not wanting to admit he had initially been rejected. And while the *Belgica*'s escape from the ice was down to him believing it could be done and then coming up with a plan to do so when everyone else thought it impossible, wasn't it this same optimism that led him to overestimate his chances of getting to the North Pole, and then the same creativity that allowed him to conjure a success so vivid he was able to convince most of the world of it, at least for a while?

So the real question is not how the hero of the *Belgica* became the liar of the North Pole, but how the hero and the liar co-existed in the same person at the same time. It is a question that gives a discordant hint at the contradictions within Cook, and in trying to explain them we can look to the poverty of his childhood, the bereavements he suffered, or the psychological effect of long months in the cold and dark. But perhaps the truth is that, while the contradictions within Cook were on a grand scale, they are the same kind of contradictions that exist in all of us.

There is another question without an answer: how would history have been different if Philip Gibbs had not happened to be in the same café as Dagmar Rasmussen, or if his news editor had chosen another journalist to send to Copenhagen? Perhaps Cook's life would have followed the same route even without Gibbs's articles. Perhaps the Peary camp's propaganda would have had the same result, and the University of Copenhagen would have still insisted on a level of proof that Cook would never have been able to produce. But while *The Times*'s claim that Gibbs had 'burst the bubble with one cable' was an exaggeration, maybe his daily articles did create enough doubt for Peary's accusations to land on more fertile ground than they would otherwise have done. Given the University of Copenhagen's rush to award Cook an honorary degree and to recommend him for the Royal Danish Geographical Society's gold medal, it seems at least possible that, without Gibbs, Cook's claim would have been accepted on trust and Peary's attacks dismissed as the jealousy of the man he had beaten across the finish line.

While the effect of Gibbs's articles on Cook's fate is debatable, their effect on Gibbs's career is clear. He arrived in Copenhagen a barely known reporter and left it one of the most famous journalists in Britain. Then, with the publication of the University of Copenhagen report, he was celebrated for the astonishing judgement and courage he had shown. This gave him a huge opportunity, which he then used to full effect by carving out a career that was among the most illustrious in the history of his profession.

But though his journalism led to an almost unprecedented level of success, journalistic successes tend to be ones that seem important at the time but then quickly fade from the public mind. While his books about the war and the political situation in Europe were well read, they, too, passed into obscurity as the politics moved on. Even his best novel, *Street of Adventure*, is now long out of print, superseded as journalists' novel of choice about their industry by books like Evelyn Waugh's *Scoop* and Michael Frayn's *Towards the End of the Morning*. In the same way, Gibbs's reporting of the Cook story may have become a Fleet Street legend, but as time passed it gradually faded from journalists' collective memory.

For all Gibbs's fame during his career, as his work was forgotten in the years after his death, so was the man. While some of the journalists he worked with, men like W.T. Stead and Alfred Harmsworth, are still remembered for the laws they campaigned to change or the newspapers they founded, Gibbs's achievements lacked this kind of durability. Today, if he is remembered at all, it is mostly for the questions around his reporting of the First World War and the Battle of the Somme. In the last few decades, journalists such as John Pilger and Philip Knightley have pointed to Gibbs as an example of their fellow reporters' long history of colluding with government propagandists, while the coverage of the centenary of the war in 2014 included the retelling of the story of Gibbs's war reporting under headlines such as 'Censorship in the trenches' and 'How state and press kept truth off the front page'.

It takes only a cursory knowledge of Gibbs's career to see that the caricature of him as a pliant client journalist does not reflect the reality of a man who risked his career in Copenhagen by challenging the conventional wisdom and who resigned from the *Daily Chronicle* in protest against the government's Irish policy. Yes, Gibbs's critics are right to say he left out details in his despatches and willingly worked under a system of censorship, but his reliance on the army for access and his desire to help Britain win the war meant his role was always going to be more complex than that of a simple chronicler of the things he saw. And as an explanation for why Gibbs wrote an article proclaiming the bloodiest day in the history of the British Army as a success, it feels inadequate. Perhaps a better explanation lies in the contradictions in Gibbs's own character that were there to see in his reporting of the Frederick Cook story seven years earlier.

The Philip Gibbs who arrived in Copenhagen was a sensitive man who was so shy that he struggled to talk to Dagmar Rasmussen on that first evening. Yet this most unlikely of reporters was transformed by the scent of the story, suddenly finding the courage to stake his whole career on him being right and the Danish scientific establishment being wrong. But while some of his reasons for doubting Cook were perceptive, his suspicion of Cook's lack of a beard feels like clutching at straws, and it is strange that he did not think it entirely natural for Cook to be nervous about approaching civilisation after so long away. Reading the articles Gibbs wrote in Copenhagen, his belief that Cook was lying feels less the result of a judicious review of the evidence and more a case of trusting his gut.

Perhaps Gibbs's pursuit of Cook was the result of an innate recklessness in him; or perhaps the lesson he learned from Copenhagen was that his intuition was a thing to be trusted, and that those who take risks tend to be rewarded. But while the courage he showed in Copenhagen passed into journalistic legend, he himself admitted the chance he took was 'too dangerous and not quite justified'. And the courage to back his own intuition would only be an asset for as long as that intuition continued to be right.

On the first day of the Battle of the Somme, he fell back on his intuition again. This time it told him that because things seemed to be going well around him, they must also be going well more widely. But the intuition that had propelled Gibbs's career to such great heights now led him to disaster. Then in the days after presenting the industrial slaughter of British soldiers as a success, the doggedness that had served him so well in Copenhagen led him to double down on a claim even after it must have been clear it might have been wrong. So just as Cook's creativity and optimism led first to him becoming the hero of the *Belgica* and later to his disgrace as the liar of the North Pole, so the courage and determination of the journalist who exposed his lie contained the seeds of failure.

It is a failure that deserves to be remembered and learned from, but it is unfair that this is often the only thing people know about Gibbs. I hope this book will play a small part in helping to bring about a more balanced view of him, so that alongside his misjudgements we also remember the brilliance of much of his journalism, the passion he brought to his work, and the fact that, as the world drifted towards war, he gave so much of himself in the cause of peace.

19

ENDINGS

Roald Amundsen: By the time Cook claimed to have reached the North Pole, Amundsen was already famous for leading the first ever expedition by boat through the Northwest Passage (connecting the Atlantic and Pacific Oceans). Then after reaching the South Pole in 1911, he led the Maud expedition, which in 1918 headed towards the North Pole. The Maud did not make it to the Pole, but it did get through the Northeast Passage, and then in 1926 Amundsen flew over the North Pole in an airship piloted by the Italian aviator Umberto Nobile. He later fell out with Nobile, but when Nobile crashed while attempting another polar flight in 1928, Amundsen, now aged 55, led a mission to rescue him and his crew. Amundsen's flying boat disappeared, presumed to have crashed. Parts of it were later discovered, but his body was never found. Cook heard the news in prison, where he was serving his sentence for fraud; long after the world at large had accepted Amundsen was dead, Cook clung to the belief that his old friend would be found alive.

Knud Rasmussen: The year after the Cook controversy, he and Peter Freuchen established a trading post at Thule in north-western Greenland. In 1921, he began the legendary Fifth Thule Expedition, a three-year, 30,000km sledge journey across the Arctic that involved visiting many Inuit communities and collecting evidence that significantly increased the world's understanding of Inuit culture (the anthropologist Elizabeth Cruwys wrote in 2003 that 'over half a century later, his writings are still regarded as some of the finest sources of ethnographic information in the Arctic'). Rasmussen was so well regarded that his speech to the International Court of Justice in The Hague in 1932 was thought to be one of the reasons Greenland came under the ownership of Denmark rather than Norway. He died in 1933, aged 54, probably as a result of eating too much fermented or rotten meat, and Danish Prime Minister Thorvald Stauning responded to his passing by calling him 'one of the best men Denmark ever bred'. *The New York Times* reported that he 'was identified with exploration in Greenland, and particularly with studies of the Eskimos, as that of no other had been'. The Knud Rasmussen Range of mountains in Greenland is named after him, and he was the subject of the 2006 Canadian–Danish film, *The Journals of Knud Rasmussen*.

Dagmar Rasmussen: She and Knud had three children together, the first born in December 1909, the month of the University of Copenhagen commission into Cook's polar claim (which means she would have been some months pregnant when she met Gibbs in the café on his first night in Copenhagen). Her and Knud's relationship became strained by Knud's long absences and his relationships with other women, and in 1929 she had an affair with the American painter Rockwell Kent. But she and Knud stayed together until Knud's death. Dagmar died in Copenhagen in 1965, aged 82. A year before her death, she had been at the unveiling of a statue of her husband a few miles outside Copenhagen by King Frederick IX, the son of Crown Prince Christian.

Crown Prince Christian: He became King Christian X of Denmark following the death of his father, Frederick VIII, in 1912. The key event of his reign was the Easter Crisis of 1920, when his decision to sack his Cabinet provoked demonstrations that put the future of the monarchy in doubt. He eventually backed down, and acted as a constitutional monarch for the rest of his reign. He regained the love and respect of the Danish public after Nazi Germany invaded Denmark in 1940; his daily horse rides through Copenhagen wearing a badge that included the Danish flag became a symbol of Danish national identity. Then, in what became known as the Telegram Crisis of 1942, he responded to a long message from Hitler congratulating him on his birthday with a perfunctory reply ('My utmost thanks, King Christian'). Hitler was so angry that it ultimately led to the Danish Government being replaced by one the Nazis thought would be more co-operative. Christian fell ill in 1942 and died in 1947.

Peter Freuchen: He continued to travel, including with Knud Rasmussen, and was for a time governor of the Thule colony in Greenland. After developing gangrene in the Arctic in 1926, he cut off his own toes using a set of nail clippers and a hammer; the whole foot was later amputated. He wrote more than 20 books, two of which were made into the 1933 film *Eskimo*, which won the first Oscar for best film editing (Freuchen also acted in it). It was at the party to celebrate the end of the filming of *Eskimo* that Freuchen caused a stir when he demonstrated his strength by lifting Hollywood star Jean Harlow and holding her at arm's length over his head. He was part of the Danish resistance during the Second World War, apparently helping to hide people from the German occupiers and eventually being forced to flee to Sweden. From there, he moved to the United States, where he gained a degree of celebrity in 1956 when he won the top prize on the television show *The $64,000 Question*. He died in 1957, aged 71. Freuchen Land in north-western Greenland is named after him.

Ernest Shackleton: By 1909, the Irish-born explorer was already a successful explorer with two Antarctic expeditions behind him. But it was his attempt to cross Antarctica between 1914 and 1916 for which he is best remembered. His ship, *Endurance*, was trapped by ice in early 1915 and then sank ten months later. Shackleton's leadership ensured the crew was able to overcome huge obstacles to get back to civilisation without a single death. He set off on a fourth Antarctic expedition in 1921, but died of a heart attack at South Georgia in 1922, aged 47. His name is now synonymous with courageous leadership.

Otto Sverdrup: Between 1914 and 1915, he led a mission to rescue two missing Arctic expeditions, and in 1917 he returned the Order of the Crown he had been awarded by the German Government, in protest at the deaths of Norwegian sailors caused by U-boats. In 1921, he led a final expedition of ships through the Kara Sea, and then in retirement he was involved in the restoration of the *Fram*, the legendary ship that had carried Nansen to his 'farthest north' record and Amundsen towards the South Pole. He died in 1930, aged 76. Sverdrup Islands in northern Canada, Sverdrup Island in Greenland, and Sverdrup Island in the Kara Sea in Russia are all named after him, and a Royal Norwegian Navy frigate, HNoMS *Otto Sverdrup*, is named in his honour.

Elis Strömgren: He continued his work at the University of Copenhagen, which included working on the calculations for Jens Olsen's World Clock, an astronomical clock that is displayed in Copenhagen City Hall. He was nominated three times for the Nobel Peace Prize for his commitment to strengthening international scientific communication, but did not win it. In 1940, he was succeeded as the director of the Royal Copenhagen Observatory by his son, Bengt, who went on to have an illustrious career as an astronomer, gaining world recognition for his research into what stars are made of. Strömgren died in Copenhagen in 1947. The asteroid 1422 *Strömgrenia* is named after him.

Alfred de Quervain: When Gibbs interviewed him, de Quervain had just returned from an expedition to Greenland, and he returned there in 1912, where he was part of a group that crossed the inland ice sheet and discovered a mountain chain they called Schweizerland. He was appointed director of the Swiss Seismological Service, was appointed professor at the University of Zürich, and played a role in establishing the Sphinx Observatory in Switzerland, one of the highest observatories in the world. He died of a stroke in 1927, aged 47. Quervain Bjerg, one of the mountains in the Schweizerland chain, and Quervain Peak in Antarctica are named after him.

Andreas Hovgaard: He died less than three months after the University of Copenhagen's judgement on Cook, in March 1910, aged 56. Several islands are named after him, including in Greenland, Antarctica, and Russia.

Carl Martin Norman Hansen: He continued travelling and writing, and together with the Danish composer Hakon Børresen wrote an opera that was set in Greenland and whose characters were all Inuit. It was performed at the Royal Opera House in Copenhagen and in the United States in 1921. He died in Copenhagen in 1947, aged 85.

Ernest Perris: The *Daily Chronicle* news editor became a close associate of Ernest Shackleton, which led to him securing the exclusive rights to news about Shackleton's *Endurance* expedition. It was to Perris that Shackleton sent the historic telegram in 1916 announcing he had arrived back in civilisation. Perris became editor of the *Daily Chronicle* when Lloyd George took control of it in 1918.

Herschel Parker: Following his 1910 expedition to McKinley that seemed to prove Cook had lied about having climbed it, Professor Parker made another attempt in 1912, this time almost reaching the top. His life then seems to have unravelled, his wife later claiming his increased drinking led to a 'subtle deterioration' in him. During the First World War, he again made headlines for his idea for an underwater searchlight for detecting submarines (which seems to have come to nothing) and for accusing the industrialist Henry Ford of stealing his idea for a 'baby submarine' (which Ford angrily denied). By 1919, he was apparently no longer living at home and depending on charity, reportedly telling his wife that he was tired of looking after her and their two children and that 'a man of my genius owes himself to mankind in general and cannot be tied down to routine'. She did not hear from him again for five years and made a court application to have their marriage dissolved. The day after the court issued a decree ending the marriage, Parker was found in Portland, Oregon. He told reporters he had discovered 'electro-chemical methods' for drawing gold from the waters of Lake Mono in California. He reportedly spent his later years living in California and died in Los Angeles in 1944, aged 76. Parker Pass in Denali National Park (the present-day name for McKinley) is named after him.

Maurice Egan: He continued as US Minister to Denmark until 1918. That year brought what was seen as the crowning achievement of his time there – the sale of the Danish West Indies (now called the United States Virgin Islands) to the United States for $25 million. He resigned due to ill health and returned to the United States, where he died in 1924, aged 71.

FURTHER READING

For more detail on the life of Frederick Cook and his rivalry with Robert Peary, I recommend *Cook and Peary: The Polar Controversy Resolved* by Robert M. Bryce. It is very long, but the story contains so much fascinating detail that it is worth the investment of time.

The story of the *Belgica* is an extraordinary one that deserves a book of its own rather than the 1,000 words I've spent telling it. Luckily, Julian Sancton has written just such a book – *Madhouse at the End of the Earth: The Belgica's Journey into the Dark Antarctic Night*. It really captures the feeling of what it was like being stuck on the *Belgica* for months on end, and is an utterly absorbing read. I would also recommend *My Attainment of the Pole*, Frederick Cook's own account of the events of 1908 and 1909. He is, of course, the ultimate unreliable narrator and the book has serious flaws, but there is something powerful about reading the first-hand account of the person at the centre of the controversy.

To learn more about the history of the quest to reach the North Pole, Fergus Fleming's *Ninety Degrees North* is a very good introduction to it.

To learn more about Philip Gibbs, a good summary is Martin C. Kerby's biography, *Sir Philip Gibbs and English Journalism in War and Peace*. The two books by Gibbs that are worth starting with are *The Pageant of the Years*, his autobiography published in 1946, and *Realities of War*, his memoir of the First World War (also known as *Now it Can Be Told*). They are by no means perfect, but there is also something about their slightly rough and ready feel that gives them a sense of immediacy and authenticity. And there's always *Street of Adventure*. There is a reason it came to be seen as the quintessential novel about Fleet Street, and it deserves to be more widely read.

In terms of books that tell the story of the other people who feature in this book, I would recommend *White Eskimo*, Stephen R. Bown's biography of Knud Rasmussen (from which most of the background information on Knud and Dagmar Rasmussen comes from), *Muckraker: The Scandalous Life and Times of Britain's First Investigative Journalist*, W. Sydney Robinson's biography of W.T. Stead, and Roald Amundsen's *My Life as an Explorer*.

ACKNOWLEDGEMENTS

Firstly, a massive thank you to the love of my life, Abigail Evans. Not only have you shown admirable forbearance in smilingly listening to my interminable anecdotes about Gibbs and Cook, but this book is much better because of your suggestion to rewrite the first three chapters. You know just how much support you've been to me over the last few years, and there's not a day that goes by when I don't feel lucky to have you.

Thanks also to my mum and dad, Dee and Brian Evans, for all their support over the years, and to Mum for reading an early draft and making suggestions that have improved it. Sadly, Dad died just before I sent the book to the publisher, and I want to record how grateful I am for all he's done for me.

And thanks to my children, Evelyn and Orson. Not only have they showed/feigned interest in my regular updates about this book's progress, but every day they bring wonder into my life. I feel very grateful to be the father of two children who are so interesting and nice.

I also want to say a big thank you to the family of Philip Gibbs, in particular Stephen Gibbs, for their support and kind permission to reproduce some of the images that I hope have helped bring my words to life. Thanks, as well, to *Politiken* for giving permission to reproduce some of its coverage, to the University of Copenhagen, and the Royal Danish Library for their help with my research, and to Stephen R. Bown and Julian Sancton for their advice. I am also grateful for being able to draw on the work of Robert M. Bryce and Martin C. Kerby on Cook and Gibbs, respectively, and Chapters 2, 14, and 16, in particular, were greatly helped by Bryce's *Cook and Peary: The Polar Controversy Resolved*. I also want to pay tribute to the British Library – a phenomenal institution that we are lucky to have and probably take for granted because it's been around for so long. This book would not have been possible without it.

Lastly, I am very grateful to Mark Beynon, Alex Boulton, Paul Middleton and The History Press for giving me the chance to tell the story of Philip Gibbs and Frederick Cook.

NOTES

Chapter 1: A Spell Upon a Man

1   Philip Gibbs, *Adventures in Journalism* (London, 1923), pp.36–7.
2   Philip Gibbs, *The Pageant of the Years* (London, 1946), p.13.
3   Ibid., p.72.
4   Gibbs, *Adventures in Journalism*, pp.2–3.
5   Basil Clarke, *My Round of the War* (London, 1917), p.8.
6   G.K. Chesterton, *Autobiography* (London, 1936).
7   Gibbs, *Adventures in Journalism*, p.36.
8   Philip Gibbs, *Street of Adventure* (London, 1929), p.15.

Chapter 2: Among the World's Great Men

1   There is more detail on the Arctic in literature in 'Literature's Arctic Obsession' by Kathryn Schulz, published in *The New Yorker*, 24 April 2017 (www.newyorker.com/magazine/2017/04/24/literatures-arctic-obsession).
2   Fergus Fleming, *Ninety Degrees North* (London, 2002), location 3622 (Kindle).
3   Ibid., location 8831 (Kindle).
4   *The New Yorker*, 17 April 2017.
5   Fleming, *Ninety Degrees North*, location 6721 (Kindle).
6   Quoted in *The New York Times*, 3 September 1909, p.3.
7   *The Times*, 2 September 1909, p.7.
8   *The New York Times*, 2 September 1909, p.8.
9   *Daily Chronicle*, 2 September 1909, p.1.
10 Robert M. Bryce, *Cook & Peary: The Polar Controversy, Resolved* (Pennsylvania, 1997), p.353.
11 *The New York Times*, 3 September 1909, p.2.
12 *Daily Mail*, 2 September 1909, p.7.
13 Bruce Henderson, *True North* (New York, 2006), pp.29–33.
14 Bryce, *Cook & Peary: The Polar Controversy, Resolved*, p.107.

15 Julian Sancton, *Madhouse at the End of the Earth: The Belgica's Journey into the Dark Antarctic Night* (London, 2021), p.112.
16 Roald Amundsen, *My Life as an Explorer* (first published in New York in 1927, this edition published in 2019), p.23.
17 Ibid., p.24.
18 Bryce, *Cook & Peary: The Polar Controversy, Resolved*, p.207.
19 *The New York Times*, 3 October 1906, p.1.
20 Wally Herbert, *Noose of Laurels* (London, 1989), p.26.

Chapter 3: Dr Cook, I Believe

1 *New York Herald*, 2 September 1909, p.1.
2 The account of Gibbs's meeting with Dagmar Rasmussen is taken from both *The Pageant of the Years* and *Adventures in Journalism*.
3 *Daily Chronicle*, 4 September 1909, p.1.

Chapter 4: The Story of the World

1 *The New York Times*, 5 September 1909, p.1.
2 *Daily Mirror*, 4 September 1909, p.3.
3 *Daily Telegraph & Courier*, 6 September 1909, p.9.
4 Ibid.
5 Gibbs, *The Pageant of the Years*, p.85.
6 Frederick Cook, *My Attainment of the Pole* (Chicago, 1913), p.467.
7 Ibid.
8 *Daily Telegraph & Courier*, 6 September 1909, p.9. The detail about the Crown Prince's car being overturned was not included in other newspapers.
9 Cook, *My Attainment of the Pole*, pp.467–8.
10 Grace Eckley, *Maiden Tribute: A Life of W.T. Stead* (Philadelphia, 2007), p.355.
11 Hugh Eames, *Winner Lose All: Dr Cook and the Theft of the North Pole* (Boston, 1973), p.114.
12 *The New York Times*, 5 September 1909, p.1.
13 Cook, *My Attainment of the Pole*, p.468.
14 Gibbs, *Adventures in Journalism*, p.44.
15 Bryce, *Cook & Peary: The Polar Controversy, Resolved*, p.360.
16 Eames, *Winner Lose All*, pp.115–18.
17 Ibid., p.118.
18 *The New York Times*, 6 September 1909, p.2.
19 *London Daily News*, 6 September 1909, p.5.
20 *The Times*, 6 September 1909, p.3.
21 Philip Gibbs, *Life's Adventure* (London, 1957), p.148.
22 Gibbs, *Adventures in Journalism*, p.7.
23 Gibbs's biographer Martin C. Kerby addresses the question of whether Gibbs was antisemitic, arguing that while in the 1930s Gibbs was sympathetic towards the Jews for how they were being treated in Germany, he was also

worried that outrage at Nazi antisemitism might be used to build support for those advocating that 'democracies should oppose Nazism even to the extent of waging war on it'. Kerby also writes that while Gibbs acknowledged the mistreatment of the Jews in Vienna following the *Anschluss*, his use of words like 'ruffians' and 'scallywags' to describe the young Austrian Nazis who persecuted them 'was an attempt to trivialise any event which might offer reason to make a stand against Hitler'. But Kerby concludes: 'It is unlikely that they indicate a strain of anti-Semitism, for as early as 1934 he was describing the German treatment of the Jews as a "hark back to the black days of medieval intolerance. It is senseless and cruel."'

24 Gibbs, *Adventures in Journalism*, p.7.

Chapter 5: Going Right After Him

1 Gibbs, *Adventures in Journalism*, p.43.
2 Gibbs, *The Pageant of the Years*, p.85.
3 Peter Freuchen, *Arctic Adventure* (London, 1936), p.24.
4 Gibbs, *The Pageant of the Years*, p.85.
5 Gibbs, *Adventures in Journalism*, pp.44–5.

Chapter 6: This Baffling Man

1 *The New York Times*, 5 September 1909, p.1.
2 Maurice Egan, *Recollections of a Happy Life* (New York, 1924), p.273.
3 *Daily Chronicle*, 6 September 1909, p.1.
4 *The New York Times*, 6 September 1909, p.2.
5 Bryce, *Cook & Peary: The Polar Controversy, Resolved*, p.363.
6 *Daily Telegraph & Courier*, 6 September 1909, p.9.
7 *The Times*, 7 September 1909, p.3.

Chapter 7: The Gravest Suspicion

1 *Daily Mail*, 7 September 1909, p.7.
2 *Daily Chronicle*, 7 September 1909, p.1.
3 *Politiken*, 7 September 1909, p.1.

Chapter 8: Realm of Fairy Tales

1 Fleming, *Ninety Degrees North*, location 5815 (Kindle).
2 John Edward Weems, *Maclean's* magazine, 13 February 1960.
3 Bryce, *Cook & Peary: The Polar Controversy, Resolved*, p.19.
4 Fleming, *Ninety Degrees North*, location 6245 (Kindle).
5 Herbert, *Noose of Laurels*, p.211.
6 Fleming, *Ninety Degrees North*, location 7434 (Kindle).

7 Herbert, *Noose of Laurels*, p.31.
8 Frederic William Wile, *News is Where You Find it* (New York, 1939), p.225.
9 Bryce, *Cook & Peary: The Polar Controversy, Resolved*, p.353.
10 *The New York Times*, 7 September 1909, p.1.
11 *Daily Mail*, 7 September 1909, p.7. It is unclear exactly which journalist Torp spoke to, or whether he issued a written statement that journalists presented as something he had said. In Gibbs's autobiography published 37 years later, Gibbs states that Torp had given his statement to a Danish press agency reporter, and it is possible this was the case. But in the *Daily Mail*, its correspondent claims to have actually spoken to Torp, and I have chosen to include this version of events, given it was written at the time.
12 The original text, written years after the event, refers to going to see the rector, but from newspaper reports it is clear Gibbs was referring to a meeting with Strömgren.
13 In *Adventures in Journalism*, Gibbs says one of these witnesses was the press agency journalist who had written the original story, but in the *Daily Chronicle* Gibbs wrote that it was an American journalist, and I have used this account because it was contemporaneous.
14 Peter Freuchen (translated by Johan Hambro), *Vagrant Viking: My Life and Adventures* (London, 1954), pp.90–2.
15 *The New York Times*, 7 September 1909, p.5.
16 Bryce, *Cook & Peary: The Polar Controversy, Resolved*, p.366.
17 *Daily Telegraph & Courier*, 8 September 1909, p.11.
18 *Daily Chronicle*, 8 September 1909, p.1.
19 Ibid.
20 *The New York Times*, 8 September 1909, p.1.
21 Bryce, *Cook & Peary: The Polar Controversy, Resolved*, p.368.
22 *The Times*, 8 September 1909, p.3.
23 Cook, *My Attainment of the Pole*, p.475.
24 *The New York Times*, 8 September 1909, p.3.
25 *The Morning Post*, 8 September 1909, p.7.

Chapter 9: The Most Amazing Man

1 *The New York Times*, 9 September 1909, p.1.
2 Ibid., p.3.
3 *Daily Chronicle*, 9 September 1909, p.1.
4 Quoted in *The Times*, 9 September 1909, p.3.
5 *London Daily News*, 10 September 1909, p.3
6 *The New York Times*, 9 September 1909, p.3.
7 Bryce, *Cook & Peary: The Polar Controversy, Resolved*, p.370.
8 *Daily Chronicle*, 9 September 1909, p.1. Unless otherwise attributed, the *Daily Chronicle* is the source for Gibbs's conversations with Cook and de Quervain. In the *Chronicle*, Gibbs spelled 'de Quervain' as 'de Querlain', but this has been changed in this book for clarity.

9   Gibbs, *Adventures in Journalism*, p.50.
10 Egan, *Recollections of a Happy Life*, pp.269–70.
11 The *Chronicle* article states 'they shall soe everything'. I have assumed this is a typo and have replaced 'soe' with 'see'.
12 *Politiken*, 9 September 1909, p.5.
13 *Daily Mirror*, 9 September 1909, p.3.
14 *Lemvig Folkeblad*, 10 September 1909, p.2.
15 *The Evening Star* (Washington DC), 9 September 1909, p.2.
16 Quoted in *The New York Times*, 6 September 1909, p.2.
17 *The New York Times*, 22 October 1909, p.2.

Chapter 10: I Show You My Hands

1   *Daily Chronicle*, 9 September 1909, p.1.
2   *Politiken*, 9 September 1909, p.5.
3   Gibbs, *Adventures in Journalism*, p.45.
4   Ibid., p.51; and *The Pageant of the Years*, p.89.
5   *Manchester Guardian*, 9 September 1909, p.6.
6   *The New York Times*, 10 November 1906, p.5.
7   *The New York Times*, 9 September 1909, p.4.
8   *London Daily News*, 10 September 1909, p.3.
9   Bryce, *Cook & Peary: The Polar Controversy, Resolved*, p.370.
10 Gibbs, *The Pageant of the Years*, p.86.
11 *Daily Chronicle*, 10 September 1909, p.1.

Chapter 11: A Wild Dream

1   Quoted in *The New York Times*, 10 September 1909, p.3.
2   *The New York Times*, 11 September 1909, p.1.
3   *Daily Telegraph & Courier*, 11 September 1909, p.11.
4   Bryce, *Cook & Peary: The Polar Controversy, Resolved*, p.374.
5   Ibid., p.373.
6   *Daily Telegraph & Courier*, 11 September 1909, p.11.
7   Quoted by Andrew A. Freeman, *The Case for Doctor Cook* (New York, 1961), p.164.
8   *The Westminster Gazette*, 18 September 1909, p.6.
9   *The Scotsman*, 13 September 1909, p.2.
10 *The Evening Star* (Washington DC), 2 October 1909, p.22.

Chapter 12: We Believe in You

1   *The Times*, 15 September 1909, p.3.
2   Bryce, *Cook & Peary: The Polar Controversy, Resolved*, p.386.
3   Cook, *My Attainment of the Pole*, p.477.

4   *The Times*, 22 September 1909, p.3.
5   Bryce, *Cook & Peary: The Polar Controversy, Resolved*, p.393.
6   *The Times*, 24 September 1909, p.3.
7   *Daily Chronicle*, 23 September 1909, p.1.
8   *The New York Times*, 24 September 1909, p.3.
9   Bryce, *Cook & Peary: The Polar Controversy, Resolved*, p.401.
10 Cook, *My Attainment of the Pole*, p.500.
11 Henderson, *True North*, p.265.
12 Bryce, *Cook & Peary: The Polar Controversy, Resolved*, p.417.
13 Fleming, *Ninety Degrees North*, location 7660 (Kindle).
14 *The New York Globe*, quoted in *The New York Times*, 15 October 1909, p.4.
15 *Daily Chronicle*, 14 October 1909, p.1
16 Bryce, *Cook & Peary: The Polar Controversy, Resolved*, p.432.
17 Ibid., p.435.
18 *The New York Times*, 17 October 1909, p.1.
19 Ibid.
20 Eames, *Winner Lose All*, pp.212–22.
21 *Daily Telegraph & Courier*, 28 November 1909, p.11.
22 *Daily Chronicle*, 13 December 1909, p.1.
23 Ibid.
24 Formally, the University of Copenhagen's governance included both a commission and a *konsistorium*, but for simplicity I have used 'commission' to describe both.

Chapter 13: His Own Foolish Acts

1   Cook, *My Attainment of the Pole*, p.550.
2   Ibid., p.16.
3   *The New York Times*, 22 December 1909, p.1.
4   *The Morning Post*, 22 December 1909, p.5.
5   *The New York Times*, 22 December 1909, p.1.
6   *The Morning Post*, 22 December 1909, p.5.
7   *Daily Telegraph and Courier*, 10 March 1910, p.11.
8   Quoted in *The Times*, 22 December 1909, p.4.
9   *London Daily News*, 23 December 1909, p.4.
10 *Reynold's News*, 26 December 1909.
11 *Weekly Dispatch*, 26 December 1909, p.3.
12 *The Times*, 22 December 1909, p.9.
13 *Daily Chronicle*, 22 December 1909, p.1.
14 Ibid., p.4.
15 *Skive Folkeblad*, 19 December 1909, p.4.
16 Gibbs, *Adventures in Journalism*, p.5.
17 *Review of Reviews*, January 1910, p.12.
18 Gibbs, *Adventures in Journalism*, pp.36–50.

Chapter 14: Setting Matters Right

1 *The Morning Post*, 24 December 1909, p.6, and *Daily Telegraph & Courier*, 27 December 1909, p.5.
2 *Lloyd's Weekly Newspaper*, 26 December 1909.
3 Bryce, *Cook & Peary: The Polar Controversy, Resolved*, p.473.
4 *The New York Times*, 20 February 1910, p.1.
5 *The New York Times*, 7 January 1910, p.4.
6 *The New York Times*, 21 May 1910, p.6.
7 *The New York Times*, 11 November 1910, p.4.
8 *The New York Times*, 9 November 1910, p.8.
9 *The New York Times*, 1 December 1910, p.1.
10 Cook, *My Attainment of the Pole*, pp.554–5.
11 *The New York Times*, 23 December 1910, p.1.
12 *The New York Times*, 26 December 1910, p.4.
13 *The New York Times*, 14 February 1911, p.6.
14 *The New York Times*, 12 August 1911, p.8.
15 *The New York Times*, 11 October 1911, p.14.
16 *The New York Times*, 25 October 1911, p.1. There is another version of events, preferred by Robert M. Bryce, that the Cook lecture was better received than this.

Chapter 15: Tides of Human Misery

1 Gibbs, *Adventures in Journalism*, p.104.
2 Gibbs, *The Pageant of the Years*, p.70.
3 *Daily Express*, 5 November 1924, p.5.
4 Wile, *News is Where You Find it*, p.224.
5 Hamilton Fyfe, *Sixty Years of Fleet Street* (London, 1949), pp.141–3.
6 Gibbs, *Adventures in Journalism*, pp.60–3.
7 Ibid., pp.75–7.
8 Gibbs, *Life's Adventure*, p.26.
9 Gibbs, *Adventures in Journalism*, p.119.
10 Gibbs, *Life's Adventure*, pp.129–30.
11 Gibbs, *Adventures in Journalism*, pp.133–41.
12 Ibid., p.189.
13 Philip Gibbs, *The Deathless Story of the Titanic* (London, 1912), p.4.
14 Gibbs, *Adventures in Journalism*, p.198. Gibbs remembers the meeting with Stead as taking place in May 1912, which must be wrong because Stead was dead by then.
15 Ibid., p.210.
16 Ibid., p.214.
17 Gibbs, *The Pageant of the Years*, p.157.

18 Clarke, *My Round of the War*, p.178.
19 Gibbs, *Life's Adventure*, p.113.
20 Gibbs, *Adventures in Journalism*, pp.242–3.
21 Gibbs, *The Pageant of the Years*, p.226.
22 Martin C. Kerby, *Sir Philip Gibbs and English Journalism in War and Peace* (London, 2016), p.188 (Kindle).
23 Gibbs, *The Pageant of the Years*, p.169.
24 *Daily Chronicle*, 3 July 1916, p.1.
25 Ibid., p.5.
26 *Daily Chronicle*, 4 July 1916, p.1.
27 *Daily Chronicle*, 5 July 1916, p.1.
28 *Daily Chronicle*, 6 July 1916, p.1.
29 *Daily Chronicle*, 10 July 1916, p.1.
30 Gibbs, *The Pageant of the Years*, p.208.
31 Gibbs, *Adventures in Journalism*, p.253.
32 Gibbs, *The Pageant of the Years*, p.226.

Chapter 16: The Psychological Enigma

1   *The New York Times*, 14 November 1911, p.5.
2   Sancton, *Madhouse at the End of the Earth*, p.290.
3   Ibid., pp.292, 294, and 353.
4   *Southwest Missourian*, 3 February 1923, p.3.
5   Amundsen, *My Life as an Explorer*, p.48.
6   *The New York Times*, 24 January 1926, p.2.
7   *The New York Times*, 25 January 1926, p.4.
8   *The Times*, 21 February 1936, p.13.
9   *The Times*, 6 August 1940, p.7.
10 *Daily Herald*, 6 August 1940, p.3.

Chapter 17: The Wounded Soul

1   Gibbs, *The Pageant of the Years*, p.233.
2   Gibbs, *Adventures in Journalism*, pp.242–3.
3   Gibbs, *The Pageant of the Years*, p.265.
4   Philip Gibbs, *Now it Can Be Told* (New York, 1920).
5   Kerby, *Sir Philip Gibbs and English Journalism in War and Peace*, p.243 (Kindle).
6   Philip Gibbs, *The Hope of Europe* (London, 1921), p.324.
7   Gibbs, *The Pageant of the Years*, pp.248 and 252.
8   Gibbs, *Adventures in Journalism*, p.266.
9   Gibbs, *The Pageant of the Years*, p.242.
10 Gibbs, *The Hope of Europe*, pp.17–18.
11 Gibbs, *Adventures in Journalism*, p.46.

12 Ibid., pp.36–51.

13 *The Westminster Gazette*, 18 September 1925, p.6.

14 Kerby, *Sir Philip Gibbs and English Journalism in War and Peace*, p.220 (Kindle).

15 Gibbs, *The Pageant of the Years*, p.353.

16 He was for a short time the editor of the *Review of Reviews*, W.T. Stead's old magazine, but he seems to have been a hands-off editor, and spent much of his time as editor giving lectures in the United States.

17 Gibbs, *The Pageant of the Years*, p.347.

18 Quoted in Kerby, *Sir Philip Gibbs and English Journalism in War and Peace*, p.232 (Kindle).

19 Philip Gibbs, *Crowded Company* (London, 1949), p.241.

20 Gibbs, *The Pageant of the Years*, p.386.

21 *The New York Times*, 3 March 1934, p.4.

22 Philip Gibbs, *Ordeal in England* (London, 1937), p.356.

23 Ibid., pp.230–4.

24 *The Times*, 18 March 1939, p.13.

25 Gibbs, *The Pageant of the Years*, p.443.

26 Philip Gibbs, *Across the Frontier* (London, 1939), quoted from the *Nottingham Journal*, 11 July 1939, p.4.

27 Kerby, *Sir Philip Gibbs and English Journalism in War and Peace*, p.276.

28 Gibbs, *The Pageant of the Years*, pp.457–8.

29 Ibid., p.518.

30 Ibid., p.529.

31 Kerby, *Sir Philip Gibbs and English Journalism in War and Peace*, p.295.

Chapter 18: Epilogue

1 Amundsen, *My Life as an Explorer*, p.137.

2 *Daily Mirror*, 8 September 1909, p.3.

3 *The New York Times*, 21 February 1920, p.4.

4 *The New York Times*, 20 February 1920, p.1.

5 Bryce, *Cook & Peary: The Polar Controversy, Resolved*, p.757.

6 *The New York Times*, 23 August 1988, p.20.

7 Andrew A. Freeman, *The Case for Dr Cook* (New York, 1961), p.164.

8 Eames, *Winner Lose All*, p.118.

9 *The New York Times*, 30 March 2008.

These notes are a selected list of sources used. They are not exhaustive, and do not include every occasion when parts of the narrative have been drawn from a mixture of the following sources, in particular: Bryce, *Cook & Peary: The Polar Controversy, Resolved*; Gibbs, *Adventures in Journalism*; Gibbs, *The Pageant of the Years*; Kerby, *Sir Philip Gibbs and English Journalism in War and Peace*; and newspaper reports of the time.

INDEX

Note: *italicised* page numbers indicate illustrations

and Rasmussen 58, 78, 82, 84, 85, 86, 143, 144–5, 198–9
Ireland 154, 178, 180

Japan 167
Jaurès, Jean 154, 157
Johansen, Hjalmar 14
The Journals of Knud Rasmussen (film) 199

Kansas 119, 146, 170
Kara Sea 201
Kent, Rockwell 199
Kerby, Martin C. 179, 186
Kipling, Rudyard 8, 10
Kitchener, Lord 157
Knightley, Philip 195
Knud Rasmussen Range, Greenland 199
Kristiansand, Norway 101, 115

Le Havre 158
Le Matin 15, 61, 85, 87
le Neve, Ethel 153
League of Nations 181
Lecointe, Georges 135
Leipzig 156
Lerwick, Shetland Islands 14, 26
Little Folks (magazine) 8
Lloyd George, David 159–60, 162, 178, 202
Lloyd's Weekly Newspaper 48
London Daily News 15, 38–9, 41
Lonsdale, Walter 124, 125, 126, 128, 129, 134, 142
Loos, Battle of 159
Loose, August Wedel 125–6, 129–31, 133
Louise, Queen 38

MacDonald, Ramsay 181
Maginot Line 185
Malaya 167
Manchester Guardian 93
Manhattan Opera House, New York 145
Manila 167
Markham, Albert 14

Marseilles 129, 141
Maud expedition to North Pole (1918) 198
McKinley, Mount (now Denali) 23–4, 64, 93–5, 120–4, 136, 141, 142–3, 144, 192, 203
Melchior (boat) 101–2, 115
Miller, Walter P. 95
Morley, Henry 14
Munich 141, 181
Murphy, Big Tim 170
My Attainment of the Pole (Cook) 145–6, 166

Nansen, Fridtjof 14, 49, 63, 69, *114*, 135–6
 'farthest north' record 49, 201
National Geographic Society 24, 64, 171, 188, 190–1
Nazism 141, 182, 200, 210n
Nepal 167
New York 106
 Cook receives freedom of 121, 122
 Cook returns to 95, 101, *111*, 115–19, 146, 191–2
 Cook's early life in 17, 22
 Daily Chronicle's correspondent in 74, 105, 117
 doubts grow in 93–4, 95, 136, 140
 Frederick A. Cook Society 192
 Gibbs in 176, 180
The New York Globe 120–1
New York Herald 22, 26–7, 33–4, 40, 53–4, 60, 69–70, 72, 105, 115, 133
New York Post 74
New York Sun 71, 94
The New York Times 15, 24, 41, 63, 69, 85–6, 171, 173–4, 191, 199
 finds Cook in Santiago 141, 189
 negative reporting on Cook's claims 71, 74, 94, 100, 122, 125, 131, 134, 136, 141
 prints Gibbs's articles 48, 65, 176, 181
New York Tribune *108*, 120, 136
New York World 117, 142